Grades 3-6

CELEBRATING
Diversity with ART

Thematic Projects for Every Month of the Year

Grades 3-6

CELEBRATING Diversity with ART

Thematic Projects for Every Month of the Year

Willet Ryder, Ed. D.

GoodYearBooks

An Imprint of ScottForesman
A Division of HarperCollinsPublishers

Dedication

To Elé and Tama Ryder, and teachers and students everywhere.

Acknowledgements

I would like to express my special thanks to Eleanor J. Ryder, Tama B. Ryder, Roberta Dempsey, Jennifer L. Bevington, Eden Sommerville, Scott Thomas, William Howe, and the staffs of the Connetquot Public Library and the Patchoque-Medford Public Library. My appreciation also to Christopher Jennison for his original interest in my educational writing.

GoodYearBooks

are available for most basic curriculum subjects plus many enrichment areas. For more GoodYearBooks, contact your local bookseller or educational dealer. For a complete catalog with information about other GoodYearBooks, please write:

GoodYearBooks
ScottForesman
1900 East Lake Avenue
Glenview, IL 60025

Book design by Street Level Studio.
Copyright © 1995 Willet Ryder.
All Rights Reserved.
Printed in the United States of America.

ISBN   0-673-36170-5

3 4 5 6 7 8 9 - BI - 03 02 01 00 99 98

TABLE
Contents

From *Celebrating Diversity with Art: Thematic Projects for Every Month of the Year*, published by GoodYearBooks. Copyright © 1995 by Willet Ryder.

Preface

Each month colors the year with special holidays and special issues. In America, home of people from all over the globe, each month is labeled to celebrate a particular subject. Some of these subjects have been recognized on a national level, while others have been named by specific groups or business organizations. As these monthly themes unfold, all of us can gain new insights into important aspects of American life. In this book, I will focus on a particular theme for each month of the year. I will begin by discussing each monthly theme with special reference to the classroom teacher (grades 3-6). Next, a group of art activities for children will be presented, in connection with each theme. These art activities are designed to spark the children's interest and increase their knowledge. Finally, additional information about follow-up experiences and helpful readings will be provided at the conclusion of each activity. One of the most difficult problems about such a book is trying to decide which monthly theme to use. Let's take the month of March as an example. This month is National Women's History Month, National Noodle Month, National Peanut Month, Poetry Month, and Irish-American Month. Needless to say, selecting a single theme wasn't an easy task! Although I personally felt that children need to be more aware of famous women from the past and in the present, I also enjoy eating noodles in many forms, love peanut butter and stories about George Washington Carver, find poetry to be fascinating, and always wear green on St. Patrick's Day. However, I believe it would be too gigantic an undertaking to focus on many different themes for each month. Thus, for the sake of cohesion and in-depth exploration, I have selected just twelve themes for the year. The twelve monthly themes are listed below:

January:	National Hobby Month	**July:**	National Recreation and Parks Month
February:	African-American History Month	**August:**	National Water Quality Month
March:	National Women's History Month	**September:**	National Hispanic Heritage Month
April:	Keep America Beautiful Month	**October:**	Family History Month
May:	Asian-Pacific Heritage Month	**November:**	National American Indian Heritage Month
June:	Zoo and Aquarium Month	**December:**	Universal Human Rights Month

Since this book is designed for teachers of mid-elementary grades, from many different regions and with many different time schedules, there is a definite need to address all twelve months. Let's take a journey then, down the road of months. It is a road well worth exploring—a byway where there is adventure and information just around the bend or over the hill!

National Hobby Month

Hobbies are both a mystery and a delight. They're a mystery because many people with hobbies don't always share them with others. They're a delight because of the pure joy they provide to the hobbyist, making hours pass like minutes! Although many hobbies are fairly common, others are quite unusual. When I was a young boy, one of the teens in the neighborhood collected tropical fish. Having an aquarium with a number of tropical fish is not uncommon. This guy, however, had about 100 fish tanks, which ranged in size from about two feet to six feet in length. My friends and I would visit him often, just to gaze in amazement at all those underwater worlds decorating his home. Each tank contained wonderful plant life, rocks, and sunken treasures, and the fish glided through these terrains in mysterious ways. There were giant angelfish and gouramis, Siamese fighting fish, and busy catfish. Pumps blew air bubbles into the watery depths as lights glimmered overhead! This guy's house was better than the local pet store, and that's no fish story!

Yet hobbies can be much simpler than my boyhood recollections of a neighbor's passion for tropical fish. My wife, Eleanor, has always been interested in stamps, for instance, and has collected some wonderful ones over the years. Although the stamps are not mounted in albums, she continues to enjoy saving attractive postage. About ten years ago, she met the late Adam Voltz, a stamp collector extraordinaire. Mr. Voltz collected stamps for a good part of his life. Each year, in an effort to stimulate her students' interest in stamp collecting, Eleanor would invite Mr. Voltz to visit her fourth-grade class to show and discuss his lifelong hobby. The children were fascinated not only by his vast collection, but also by his great stories and charismatic personality. As a result, many of my wife's students have become avid stamp collectors. The main thrust of National Hobby Month is to share special information about and increase knowledge of various hobbies. Not everyone can pursue every hobby, of course, but each of us can benefit by learning a little bit about some of them. In this section of the book, we will focus on art activities that are based on a selection of potential hobbies. Each activity will consist of just a tiny taste of something new—hopefully, whetting the children's appetite for a larger serving.

THE ROCKY ROAD

The quartz crystal glimmers on the tiny shelf, a gift from my daughter's friend, Kathleen Prime. It rests next to a fluorite crystal, which I once bought at a museum. Rocks and minerals are fascinating things and are lots of fun to find, study, and display. Anyone who has ever walked along the shore of an ocean, bay, river, or lake knows that such places can be real "rocky" delights! Streams and brooks also often bubble over with a variety of rock treasures. Rocks and pebbles situated along the water are generally smoothed and polished by natural forces and are fairly easy to find and collect. Many other rocks and minerals are found in the earth and have to be dug out or mined. Rocks and minerals provide a glimpse of our earth's ancient past and serve as indicators that the physical world is constantly changing. Before starting this activity with your class, a visit to the library or to a nearby natural history museum is strongly recommended. It's a good idea to get hold of a set of mineral samples and some hand lenses or magnifying glasses so that the kids can study the rocks more closely.

Materials

- rock and mineral sets
- hand lenses or magnifying glasses
- 8" x 11" composition paper
- 9" x 12" manila paper
- pencils
- crayons

Activity

1. Show some posters and/or books about rocks and minerals, and ask the children how these things form. Where do they come from? What natural forces (for example, water, heat, etc.) help to create them?

2. Distribute some sample rocks and minerals along with the hand lenses and magnifying glasses, and ask the children to carefully study them.

3. Supply the children with 8" x 11" composition paper, and request that they record such things as color, shape, and texture.

4. Next, distribute the 9" x 12" manila paper, pencils, and crayons, and ask each child to carefully draw one of the rock/mineral samples. Be sure each child correctly labels the sample shown in her/his drawing.

5. Last, dispense more 9" x 12" manila paper, and ask the children to imagine that they are on a rock-finding adventure and to draw a scene using both real and imaginary rocks and minerals. Such scenes could include giant caves, old mines, and the like.

6. When the drawings are complete, hold a sharing session and exhibit.

Follow-Up

A real rock collector, from outside the school, is always a treat. If you know of a master rock collector, don't hesitate to invite him/her in for a class visit! In addition, encourage the children, who may have their own rock collections at home, to bring them to class for discussion and exhibit.

Helpful Books

- Bullis, Douglas. *Crystals: The Science, Mysteries, and Lore.* New York: Crescent Books, 1990.
- Hiscock, Bruce. *The Big Rock.* New York: Atheneum, 1988.
- Pellant, Chris. *Rocks and Minerals.* New York: Dorling Kindersley, 1992.
- Shedenhelm, W. R. C. *The Young Rockhound's Handbook.* New York: Putnam's, 1978.

3

WHAT'S COOKING?

One very tasty hobby is cooking! Anyone who enjoys licking icing bowls, hanging around kitchens, and sampling goodies will probably enjoy cooking. Cooking can be divided into many categories. These include appetizers; soups and salads; main dishes; side dishes; breads; rolls and pastries; and desserts. Ummm! I'm getting hungry just writing these down! Chefs usually specialize in just one of these food areas, often becoming famous for their pastries, salads, or main entrees!

Before introducing this activity to the class, prepare a simple appetizer, from your favorite home recipes, and bring it to school.

Materials

- your appetizer
- paper plates
- napkins
- 8" x 11" composition paper
- 12" x 18" manila paper
- pencils
- crayons
- markers

Activity

1. Serve your appetizer on paper plates, and let the children sample it. After they have completed their sampling, distribute the composition paper and pencils, and ask students to write a brief paragraph about how the food tasted. You might supply the class with a few descriptive words to help stimulate ideas (for example: spicy, bland, smooth, exciting, etc.).

2. Next, pass out the 12" x 18" manila paper, pencils, crayons, and markers, and ask each child to draw his/her own culinary creation. Try to have the students focus on one item, such as the largest and fanciest cake, the biggest serving of spaghetti and meatballs, or the most colorful fruit salad.

3. When the art works are complete, hold a discussion and exhibition.

Follow-Up

Creating your own class cookbook is a fantastic way to expand on this activity. First, invite each child to bring in a recipe from home, which he/she loves! Collect the recipes, and file them under the different food categories discussed earlier. Next, ask the children to make simple illustrations for their recipes using black marker. The class might also wish to choose a few children to illustrate the cover of the cookbook. Finally, type up the recipes and paste the illustrations in place. Then photocopy, collate, and bind the entire work. Make sure that each child receives a copy and that you have extra copies for the school library and for interested friends and relatives. Needless to say, you and your class may wish to sample some of these recipes during the school year. Enjoy and *bon appétit*!

Helpful Books

- Greene, Karen. *Once Upon a Recipe.* New Hope, PA: New Hope Press, 1987.
- Hayes, Phyllis. *Food Fun.* New York: Franklin Watts, 1981.
- Krementz, Jill. *The Fun of Cooking.* New York: Alfred A. Knopf, 1985.
- Oetker, Dr. August. *Let's Cook.* New York: Sterling Publishing, 1993.

From *Celebrating Diversity with Art: Thematic Projects for Every Month of the Year,* published by GoodYearBooks. Copyright © 1995 by Willet Ryder.

Sewing:
A Stitch in Time

Sewing and stitchery can be more than just "sew-sew," it can be great! Without all those skillful stitches, our clothes would fall apart and our buttons would be constantly falling off. This activity is not designed, however, to make us into tailors or clothing designers, but rather to increase our appreciation of the wonderful art of creative sewing. Many museums of folk art contain exhibits of creative stitchery. Some of these designs are abstract, while others are based on patterns handed down from generation to generation. The key to approaching a sewing activity is to think of sewing as a journey into design—one involving a thread and needle rather than a pencil or paintbrush!

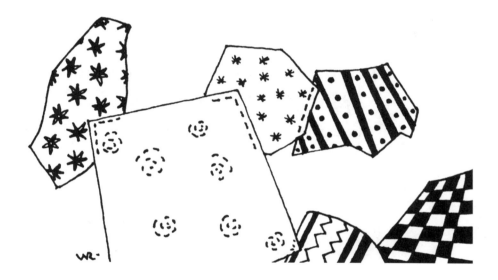

Materials

- lots of scrap fabric with varied colors and textures
- thread (varied colors)
- needles
- scissors
- straight pins
- thimbles

Activity

1. Collect a batch of varied fabric scraps, with different patterns, colors, and textures, and bring them to class. A local fabric store may be happy to donate some of their scraps to your class.

2. Show the class some pictures or actual examples of creative stitchery designs and discuss.

3. Explain about threading needles and working safely and carefully.

4. Let each child choose, cut, and arrange several pieces of fabric and try some different stitches using threads of various colors. Encourage the children to experiment with their cutting and sewing.

5. After the children finish their creative designs, display their works.

Follow-Up

Invite a skilled stitchery artist to your class to show her/his work and talk to your students. You might also consider visiting a craft museum where sewing is displayed. Some restored historical villages, such as Old Bethpage Village on Long Island, have special tours for children, allowing them the opportunity to play tailor's apprentice for a few hours. Such an outing will keep the whole class on "pins and needles."

Helpful Books

- Barkin, Carol, and James, Elizabeth. *Slapdash Sewing.* New York: Lothrop, Lee & Shepard Company, 1975.
- Corrigan, Barbara. *I Love to Sew.* Garden City, NY: Doubleday, 1974.
- Corrigan, Barbara. *Of Course You Can Sew!* Garden City, NY: Doubleday, 1971.
- Encinas, Lydia Proenza. *A Beginner's Book of Sewing.* New York: Dodd, Mead, 1977.
- Katz, Ruth J. *Make It and Wear It.* New York: Walker and Company, 1981.

From *Celebrating Diversity with Art: Thematic Projects for Every Month of the Year,* published by GoodYearBooks. Copyright © 1995 by Willet Ryder.

STAMP COLLECTING

Anyone who has ever visited a local post office has no doubt noticed the fantastic variety of stamps made by the U.S. Postal Service. Those of us who have received a letter or card from another country have probably spent a moment or two studying the strange stamp. Collecting stamps is a true adventure in color and design. It's a wonderful way to let one's mind wander and imagine different times and far away places! In this activity, we will be focusing on this special hobby, introducing children to the amazing world of stamps.

Materials

- 9" x 12" newsprint and white drawing paper
- pencils
- rulers
- markers
- watercolors
- newspaper
- cans
- brushes
- water

Activity

1. Start the activity by inviting each child to bring an interesting stamp to class. You might bring in a batch of stamps as well, in case the children forget.

2. Invite children to discuss what they notice about their stamps. What kind of information does a stamp contain? You might make a list of these items on the chalkboard.

3. Next, ask each child to imagine that she/he is a stamp artist who has been asked to design a special stamp for any country of her/his choice.

4. Pass out the newsprint paper, and have the children make sketches of their designs.

5. Have each child choose his/her favorite design and enlarge and transfer it to the 9" x 12" white drawing paper, using pencil and ruler.

6. Children can color the final designs using markers and watercolors.

7. Exhibit these large stamps in the school or at the local post office.

Follow-Up

Invite a stamp collector or a member of the local post office to your classroom to discuss stamp collecting. Be sure to ask them to bring all or part of their collection to show the class. Stamp collectors are usually very happy to introduce young people to their hobby. Take, for example, the late Adam Voltz, who used to visit my wife's fourth-grade class each year. Mr. Voltz has given many young collectors their start with his great collection and interesting stories!

Helpful Books

- Allen, Judy. *Stamps and Stamp Collecting.* Tulsa, OK: Hayes Books, 1981.
- Briggs, Michael. *Stamps.* New York: Random House, 1992.
- Chapman, Kenneth, and Baker, Barbara. *All Color Book of Stamps.* London: Octopus Books, 1974.
- Hobson, Burton. *Getting Started in Stamp Collecting.* New York: Sterling Publishing, 1982.
- Hobson, Burton. *Stamp Collecting as a Hobby.* New York: Sterling Publishing, 1986.
- Martin, M.W. *Topical Stamp Collecting.* New York: Arco Publishing, 1975.

From *Celebrating Diversity with Art: Thematic Projects for Every Month of the Year,* published by GoodYearBooks. Copyright © 1995 by Willet Ryder.

COIN COLLECTING

When the salesclerk plunked the coins in my hand, I remember thinking that something about the change looked different! When I opened my hand to peer at each coin more closely, I realized that one of the coins was Canadian. I was a young boy living in upstate New York at the time, so the odds of getting a smattering of coins from that big country to the north of us were quite high. Yet encountering a coin with a different design representing another country was truly exciting. For coins symbolize the lure and adventure of other places—often far from one's doorstep! I suspect that many people also collect coins because they aren't too large and are always worth something.

The purpose of this activity is to get children to study and appreciate the world of coins. In preparation, try to gather some coins from other lands to show the class. If you don't have such a collection, you can begin by showing students a variety of American coins. Don't forget to mention that many coin collectors are on the lookout searching for American coins from certain years or with specific flaws.

Materials

- sample coins
- 8" x 11" unlined composition paper
- pencils (#2)

Activity

1. Pass around the sample coins so that the class can study them more closely. You might provide the children with some study questions to answer about each coin. Questions might include the following: How large is the coin? What color is it? How old is it? What is the primary design on each side of the coin? Is the coin

worn or well preserved? Such questions will encourage the children to more carefully focus their attention on the coins they are examining.

2. Briefly discuss the children's answers to the study questions.

3. Next, have the children gather around you, so that they can watch you make a rubbing of one of the coins:

   a. First, place your coin under a clean sheet of unlined paper.

   b. Then, hold a #2 sharpened pencil nearly parallel to the surface of the paper and gently rub over the area covering the coin. Begin with the edges first, and then rub toward the center.

   c. As the design of the coin begins to appear, you can increase the contrast by putting more pressure on the pencil point. Be careful to always use the side of the point and not to press too hard.

   d. Explain that different coins can be placed in different parts of the paper to create various designs.

4. Finally, let each child select a coin from the batch you brought in, or from his/her pocket or purse. After choosing the coin they want, ask them to make a rubbing of it using the above technique.

5. Hold a sharing session and exhibit when the rubbings are complete.

Follow-Up

In an effort to enhance this topic, contact a local coin collector to make a class visit and explain her/his collection. In addition, you might take the class on a field trip to a local museum that includes a coin collection. If you live near a U.S. Mint, such as the Franklin Mint in Philadelphia, arrange a class visit.

Helpful Books

• Krause, Chester L., Mishler, Clifford, & Bruce II, Colin R. (ed.) *Standard Catalog of World Coins*. Iola, WI: Krause Publications, 1991.

TRAINS: KEEPING ON TRACK

Whenever I hear a train whistle, I think about the adventure of travel by rail. Anyone who has ever climbed aboard a train knows the wonderful feeling of embarking on a journey—even if it's just to the next town down the line. To celebrate the lore of trains, model train sets have been designed that often duplicate their giant counterparts down to the smallest detail. Perhaps some of us have received train sets as a holiday or birthday present. Did you know that some really avid model train enthusiasts even wear engineer caps when running their sets?

Model trains can be truly marvelous to look at! Toy and hobby shops often have excellent displays, which might include mountains, tiny towns, and shrubbery. In this activity, we will honor the hobby of model train collecting and the hobbyists who help keep them on the track!

Before starting this activity, ask the children to bring some empty half-gallon milk or juice cartons to class. It's important that these cartons be thoroughly rinsed! In addition, ask the kids to collect and bring in plastic bottle caps and pieces of corrugated cardboard from boxes. After you have assembled these materials, you're ready to begin.

Materials

- clean half-gallon milk or juice containers
- pieces of corrugated cardboard
- plastic bottle caps and found objects
- construction paper of assorted colors
- scissors
- white glue
- markers
- paper fasteners
- yarn or string

12

Activity

1. Start the activity by showing a model train set and/or asking how many children own their own set.

2. Show some pictures or posters of trains, and ask students what they notice.

3. Hold a brief discussion about the various parts of a train (for example, the engine, the freight and passenger cars, and the caboose).

4. Ask each student to decide which part of the train he/she wishes to make.

5. Once everyone has decided, have students cover their milk carton with construction paper of assorted colors. For best results, it's easier to cover each side of the carton separately, using white glue, rather than wrapping it like a gift.

6. Cut cardboard circles for wheels and affix with paper fasteners.

7. Decorate each car with as much detail as possible, using construction paper and found objects. The cars can be hooked together using yarn or string.

8. Assemble your class train and display it in your room or in the school library.

Follow-Up

Invite a model train hobbyist to speak to your class and show her/his model railroad. If you don't know of such a person, you might try contacting a local hobby shop where train sets are sold.

Helpful Books

- Edmonson, Harold A. *The ABC's of Model Railroading.* Milwaukee, WI: Kalmbach Publishing, 1978.
- Herda, D. J. *Model Railroads.* New York: Franklin Watts, 1982.
- Pierce, Jack. *The Freight Train Book.* Minneapolis: Carolrhoda Books, 1980.
- Radlauer, Edward, and Radlauer, David. *Model Trains.* Chicago: Childrens Press, 1979.
- Steele, Philip. *Trains.* New York: Crestwood House, 1991.
- Yepsen, Roger. *Train Talk.* New York: Pantheon Books, 1983.

13

The varied contributions of African-Americans have helped enrich the United States in a multitude of ways. From the invention of the stoplight to the creation of blood banks, from the soles of shoes to the soul of jazz, from peanut butter to the painter's easel, African-Americans have made truly outstanding contributions to our world. Unlike many immigrant groups who came freely to this country seeking a better way of life, the majority of African-Americans were brought to these shores in chains and suffered tremendous deprivations under the bonds of slavery.

During African-American History Month, we will investigate a small sampling of topics that help to define the unique qualities and achievements of the African-American people. We will begin by learning about and creating *kente* cloth and ceremonial masks. We will sculpt small goldweights and make a Senegal hat. We will also study some distinguished African-Americans who have contributed to our country. Finally, we will sample some cooking based on the yam. The suggested activities are filled with fascinating facts and fun. They are designed to increase our understanding and enlarge our knowledge of African-Americans' many accomplishments. So *karibu* (the Swahili term for "welcome") to the month that honors African-Americans!

KENTE CLOTH

Kente cloth is a cloth of beautiful colors and patterns produced in many countries of West Africa. The Ashanti people of Ghana are especially known for this woven cloth. Because of its wonderful designs and varied colors and textures, *kente* cloth is prized for its richness and cultural associations. In our own country, ties, shirts and hats are often made from such cloth. Although we will not be weaving the cloth, we will be designing original patterns, using construction paper of assorted colors and markers, that simulate the look of the cloth.

Materials

- 12" x 18" construction paper of assorted colors and scrap paper
- 12" x 18" newsprint
- pencils
- rulers
- scissors
- crayons
- markers
- white glue

Activity

1. Begin this activity by showing some samples or pictures of kente cloth and explaining where such cloth originates. Using a world map, locate West Africa and name a few West African countries.

2. Explain that each person will be designing her/his own piece of kente cloth using construction paper of assorted colors. Point out that the majority of kente cloth has geometric designs—ones generally based on the rectangle and square.

3. Ask each child to make some sketches of cloth designs, using the newsprint paper and pencils, and to select her/his favorite sketch.

15

Once the children have done so, have them color in the sketches using crayons. Remind the children not to spend too much time on the coloring, since these are just prelimary sketches!

4. When the crayon design is completed, ask each child to begin his/her final work using construction paper of assorted colors. Children should begin by selecting a single background color, then use other colors to enhance it. Each color can be cut to different widths and glued in different directions onto the background.

5. You might remind the children that a little glue goes a long way. Remember that white glue is not maple syrup!

Follow-Up

When the designs are complete and the glue has dried, hold a kente cloth display in the classroom or library. If you live near an African-American gift shop, you might invite the owner to come to class to speak to the children about kente cloth. There are also some fine books on this topic, which you can recommend to the class.

Helpful Books

- Corwin, Judith Hoffman. *African Crafts.* New York: Franklin Watts, 1990.
- Mendez, Phil. *The Black Snowman.* New York: Scholastic, 1989.

LARGE MASKS

Masks made by the peoples of African countries have both ceremonial power and magical meaning. Skillfully carved masks are used to cover elders, and often represent strong spiritual forces in nature. Although different peoples from different countries employ a variety of designs, many masks use strong geometric patterns and abstract features. Carvers sometimes embellish their work with fine linear details and wonderful motifs based on plants and animals. In this activity, we will be creating large masks based on some of the design ideas that we can see in masks from Africa.

Materials

- 12" x 18" newsprint paper
- pencils
- large pieces of corrugated cardboard
- scissors
- white glue
- construction paper of assorted colors and scrap paper
- markers
- assorted colors of tempera paint
- brushes
- water
- newspapers
- water cups and cans
- found objects

Activity

1. After gathering the materials, and some books, pictures, and/or slides about African masks, make a presentation to the class. Discuss why masks are important and what purposes they serve among African peoples. Point out the use of geometric shapes and lines.

2. Next, pass out the newsprint paper and ask each child to make a sketch of a mask that emphasizes a feeling, such as happiness,

17

sadness, joy, fear, or surprise. Encourage them to use geometric shapes and decorative lines.

3. After the sketches are complete, group the children in teams of four, and have each group select one mask design from its members.

4. When the designs have been selected, pass out the large pieces of cardboard, and ask each group to expand on its sketch by cutting out the mask shapes from the cardboard provided. Remember that sections of the mask can be built up, in a relief fashion, using pieces of cardboard cut and glued to the main mask design. The top layer of cardboard can be peeled back to expose the linear corrugations underneath. This will also give the mask an interesting texture.

5. After the cardboard work is done, the masks can be decorated using construction paper of assorted colors, markers and tempera paints. Encourage children to work carefully, reminding them that this is a team effort. When the paint is dry, found objects, such as buttons, sequence, pipe cleaners, and feathers, can glued to the masks.

Follow-Up

An exhibit and discussion of African masks could be held once the masks are complete. Invite a lower grade class to see the work and hear student explanations. If you live near a museum that has African masks on display, organize a field trip there as a culminating activity.

Helpful Books

- Bartok, Mira, and Ronan, Christine. *Ancient and Living Cultures: West Africa: Ghana.* Glenview, IL: GoodYearBooks, 1993.
- Corwin, Judith Hoffman. *African Crafts.* New York: Franklin Watts, 1990.
- Cosner, Sharon. *Masks Around the World.* New York: David McKay, 1979.
- Dayrell, Elphinstone. *Why the Sun and the Moon Live in the Sky.* New York: Scholastic, 1968.
- Glubok, Shirley. *The Art of Africa.* New York: Harper & Row, 1965.
- Price, Christine. *The Mystery of Masks.* New York: Scribner's, 1978.
- Ryder, Willet. *The Art Experience.* Glenview, IL: GoodYearBooks, 1991.

GOLDWEIGHTS

In some African countries, gold is of special value, just as it is in the United States. Among the Ashanti people of Ghana, however, gold is a sacred metal, one associated with royalty. In order to weigh the gold, tiny weights are used on a balance scale. Each of these weights equals a certain number of ounces. Often, the goldweights are created in the shape of people, birds, animals, and insects; and sometimes possess a humorous quality. Remember that goldweights are like tiny sculptures, which means that each class member will have to work "very small!"

Materials

- 9" x 12" newsprint paper
- pencils
- plasticine
- toothpicks
- gold or brass acrylic paint
- small brushes
- cups
- water
- paper towels

Activity

1. Before introducing this activity in class, complete a few goldweights of your own at home. (Use the procedure outlined in the following steps.)

2. Show the children your goldweights and explain how they are used. If the children have never seen a balance scale, bring one to class and briefly explain its function.

3. Distribute the newsprint paper and pencils, and ask each child to sketch her/his own goldweight design. Remind the children that such weights often came in the form of a person, bird, animal, or insect.

4. When the sketch is complete, give each child another sheet of newsprint, a small piece of plasticine, and several toothpicks. Ask each student to sculpt his/her design using the pencil sketch as a model. The primary design can be pinched and sculpted out of the

plasticine with the fingers. Details can be added by applying small clay balls and embellishing the sculpture with a toothpick.

5. After the plasticine models are complete, let them dry for a day or so, to a leather-hard state. Then, squeeze a little metallic acrylic paint into the paint cups (every two students can share one cup), and distribute newsprint paper (to place beneath the sculpture), brushes, water, and paper towels.

6. Instruct children to carefully paint their tiny sculpture using the acrylic paint. Since this paint dries quickly, and the sculptures are very small, the students may wish to give their work two coats of paint.

Follow-Up

Holding a tiny goldweight exhibit would be lots of fun. A lighted showcase, if one exists in the school hallway, would be a fine place to display your goldweights. Arranging the display around a balance scale might also be interesting. Be sure to include a short written commentary on how goldweights are used.

Helpful Books

- Bartok, Mira, and Ronan, Christine. *Ancient and Living Cultures: West Africa: Ghana.* Glenview, IL: GoodYearBooks, 1993.
- Corwin, Judith Hoffman. *African Crafts.* New York: Franklin Watts, 1990.
- Glubok, Shirley. *The Art of Africa.* New york: Harper & Row, 1965.
- Plass, Margaret Webster. *African Miniatures.* New York: Frederick A. Praeger, 1967.

SENEGAL HATS

Several years ago, while walking along a crowded stretch of Jamaica Avenue in Jamaica, New York, I bought a nicely embroidered hat from a street merchant near 170th Street. Commonly called a Senegal hat, in honor of its country of origin, this type of African hat is also known as a kufi, fez, or crown. Although the designs on my hat are floral, they are somewhat abstract and stylized. In addition to the fine designs, the wonderful color combinations make these hats fun to look at and to wear!

Materials

- 9" x 12" newsprint paper
- 12" x 18" construction paper of assorted colors and scrap paper
- white glue
- rulers
- pencils
- markers
- crayons
- scissors
- staplers

Activity

1. Using a sheet of 12" x 18" construction paper, have students measure and cut two 2.5" x 18" strips.

2. They can staple or glue these strips together, forming a long band approximately 34" in length.

3. Have each student place this band around her/his head and adjust the ends so that it fits, then staple or glue the ends in the correct spot. The main band of the hat is now formed!

4. Next, ask students to sketch some floral or geometric designs on newsprint paper with pencil. Then, have them select two or three sheets of construction paper of assorted colors, and transfer their designs to these. Remind them that they can cut out a few designs at the same time by folding over the paper several times. Make sure students' designs are smaller than 2.5" in height.

5. When students have cut out a number of designs in various colors, they can attach these to the band of the hat using white glue.

6. Once the band is filled with designs, they are ready to make the crown (top) of your hat. They should begin by placing the band of the hat on edge on a piece of 9" x 12" construction paper. Holding the band down carefully, they should then use a pencil to gently trace around the inside of the band. This will create the circle for the crown of the hat.

7. Next, tell students to carefully cut out the crown and set it aside for a few moments. Then, have them measure and cut out a 2" x 9" strip of paper and cut it into small pieces. Each piece should be about 3/4" x 2". Once students have cut eight pieces, tell them to fold each piece in half (3/4" x 1"), and glue it to the band of the hat. When they are sure that the unglued section is bent toward the inside of the hat and is even with the top of the band, they are ready to glue all eight tabs, placing them at regular intervals around the band.

8. While the tabs are drying, you can decorate the crown of the hat, using the same method as described in steps 4 and 5. However, your designs can be larger than 2.5" in height.

9. When the designs have been cut, have students glue them to the hat crown. Then, using markers, they can further decorate the band and crown before gluing them together.

10. To glue the crown to the band, tell students to place a little glue on the top of each tab. Then, place the crown on their desktop with the design side down, and flip over the band so that the glued tabs are in contact with the crown. They can gently press each tab onto the crown, evening out the crown and band before the glue dries. Congratulations! You are now the proud owners, and designers of an original Senegal hat!

Follow-Up

Hold a "West African Senegal Hat Day," and have your class model their hats for the rest of the school. You may wish to arrange for a hat display, using a showcase in the school library or hallway. If you set up such a display, be sure to include a map that shows where Senegal is located, so that viewers can also sharpen their geography skills!

Helpful Books

• Severn, Bill. *Here's Your Hat.* New York: David McKay, 1963.

From *Celebrating Diversity with Art: Thematic Projects for Every Month of the Year,* published by GoodYearBooks. Copyright © 1995 by Willet Ryder.

PORTRAITS OF FAMOUS AFRICAN-AMERICANS

African-Americans have contributed to a wide range of fields which affect the lives of all of us. An astounding list of names, many of these unknown to the majority of Americans, unfolds before our eyes if we do just a bit of investigation. Consider, for example, the contributions of Louis Armstrong, Crispus Attucks, Benjamin Banneker, Mary McLeod Bethune, Gwendolyn Brooks, Dr. George Washington Carver, Shirley Chisholm, Dr. Charles Drew, Duke Ellington, Langston Hughes, Rev. Jesse Jackson, Mahalia Jackson, Dr. Martin Luther King, Jr., Jacob Lawrence, Thurgood Marshall, Elijah McCoy, Garrett Morgan, Rosa Parks, Sojourner Truth, Harriet Tubman, Phillis Wheatley, and Malcolm X. The list can go on and on!

This activity is devoted to furthering students' knowledge of notable African-Americans. To do so more effectively, you may wish to make a trip to the library before introducing the activity. After assembling a collection of books, pictures, and posters, you are ready to begin.

Materials	• 9" x 12" newsprint and white drawing paper	• pencils
	• 12" x 18" construction paper of assorted colors	• crayons
		• markers
		• scissors
		• staplers

Activity

1. You might start the activity by listing the names of a number of famous African-Americans on the chalkboard, and asking the children to identify them. You may need to do some prompting, since many children will not have heard of some of these people.

2. Show the students the pictures and books you gathered about famous African-Americans. Ask the children why they think we know so little about these people.

3. Ask each student to select one individual from the resources provided and to create a portrait of that person. Keep in mind that the portrait does not have to be realistic in style. It can be abstract and can include designs which refer to the person's achievements.

4. Distribute the newsprint paper and pencils, and ask each child to begin making a sketch of the individual she/he selected.

5. When the sketch is completed, the children should transfer it to the white drawing paper and color it using crayons and markers.

6. Backgrounds of construction paper of assorted colors can be prepared by folding the 12" x 18" sheets in half and cutting the edges into curved or angular patterns. When the paper is unfolded, students can center and staple the portrait to this paper.

7. Display the portraits, including a brief written description of the person's contributions stapled beneath each.

Follow-Up

Ask the children to write longer compositions about the people they selected and have them read their work to the class.

Helpful Books

- Adler, David A. *A Picture Book of Martin Luther King, Jr.* New York: Scholastic, 1989.

- Freeborne, Gerald L., ed. *Black History Month: A Reflection and Recognition of the African American Family.* Albany, NY: The State Education Department, 1985.

- Hoffman, Mary. *Amazing Grace.* New York: Scholastic, 1991.

- Ingraham, Leonard W. *Slavery in the United States.* New York: Franklin Watts, 1968.

- Smead, Howard. *The Afro-Americans.* New York: Chelsea House Publishers, 1989.

- Spangler, Earl. *The Blacks in America.* Minneapolis, MN: Lerner Publications, 1971.

- Stein, R. Conrad. *The Story of the Underground Railroad.* Chicago: Childrens Press, 1981.

- Winter, Jeanette. *Follow the Drinking Gourd.* New York: Alfred A. Knopf, 1988.

THE YAM

Many of us have enjoyed whipped sweet potatoes baked with marshmallow topping at a Thanksgiving feast or a festive meal. This sweet dish is a specialty of my mother-in-law, Connie Siegel. Sweet potatoes and yams are wonderful vegetables, indeed, and can be served in many different ways. In some African nations, such as Nigeria, the cultivation of yams is big business. These vegetables are an important staple of many African diets. Moreover, many African-Americans make use of yams in their cooking. One marvelous creation is sweet potato pie! This pie, for those who haven't sampled it, is sweeter and lighter than pumpkin pie, and very tasty indeed. In this activity, we will celebrate the yam by learning more about it.

Materials

- 9" x 12" construction paper of assorted colors (including orange and brown)
- scrap construction paper
- scissors
- white glue
- pencils
- markers

Activity

1. Begin the activity by talking about the yam and showing the class some yams from the supermarket or vegetable stand. Ask the children if they have eaten yams and, if so, in what form. Discuss the fact that these vegetables are an important food in many countries.

2. Next, ask the students to create yam people using construction paper of assorted colors. Distribute an orange and brown sheet to each student, and also make available a selection of colorful scraps.

3. After receiving the paper, have the children draw their yam shapes on the orange or brown sheets using pencil. When the drawings

25

are complete, pass out the scissors, and let everyone cut out their yam people.

4. Eyes, noses, mouths, mustaches, etc. can be designed and cut from the scrap sheets and glued on to the yam people. Don't forget to cut out some shoes or sneakers, so the yam people can get about! Extra touches can be added by using the markers.

5. When the yam people are complete, hold a display of these half-baked creations. It's a sweet thing to do!

Follow-Up

Ask the children to collect recipes which use yams, and compose a yam cookbook. Bake a sweet potato pie, and let the children sample it! A fine recipe for such a pie, provided to me by my friend Jeannette Kittles, is as follows:

Sweet Potato Pie

Ingredients

- 2 or 3 medium yams (cooked and then peeled)
- 1/2 cup butter
- 1/4 cup granulated sugar
- 1/4 cup firmly packed brown sugar
- 1/4 tsp. salt
- 1/4 tsp. nutmeg
- 2 eggs (well beaten)
- 1 cup milk
- 1 tsp. lemon extract
- 1 9" unbaked pie shell

Directions

- Combine butter, sugar, and nutmeg in a large bowl. Beat at medium speed until creamy.
- Beat in yams until well mixed.
- Slowly add eggs, milk, and lemon extract. Mix until creamy.
- Pour mixture into a 9" unbaked pie shell.
- Bake at 350° for 30 minutes.
- Remove from oven and cool. Can be served with various toppings, such as meringue, walnuts, etc. Enjoy!

Helpful Books

- Bourgeois, Paulette. *The Amazing Potato Book.* Reading, MA: Addison-Wesley, 1991.
- Dodge, Bertha S. *Potatoes and People.* Boston: Little, Brown, 1970.
- Haley, Gail E. *A Story A Story.* New York: Atheneum Childrens Books, 1970.
- Meltzer, Milton. *The Amazing Potato.* New York: HarperCollinsPublishers, 1992.
- Musgrove, Margaret. *Ashanti to Zulu.* New York: A Pied Piper Book, 1976.
- Silverstein, Alvin and Virginia B. *Potatoes: All About Them.* Englewood Cliffs, NJ: Prentice-Hall, 1976.

The contributions of women to both our country and the world are truly amazing, yet many people—both young and old—are unaware of them. In recent years, information on the vast achievements of women has been increasing. We still have a long way to go, however!

Women have played a significant role in every field of human endeavor. Given their numerous contributions, we can but scratch the surface by providing a small sample of people and accomplishments. It is sad indeed that we do not simply recognize the importance of all people, regardless of their gender or ethnicity. Until such a day arrives, however, it is especially important to pay tribute to some of those who have gone unrecognized. A month celebrating National Women's History enables us to do just that. During this month, we will take up the struggle for women's rights, learn about the achievements of women in various fields of endeavor, design quilt patches, and investigate the Statue of Liberty. We will use art to connect us to these vital and exciting people and events, building new understanding of and appreciation for women's many and continued contributions.

WOMAN'S SUFFRAGE

The right to vote is one of our most precious liberties. Yet for many years in our country, women were denied this basic right. Then in marched Susan B. Anthony, who mobilized women and championed their right to vote. This famous movement became known as Woman's Suffrage. Although women have made great strides since that time, there is still much to be done—especially with regard to electing women to high office. Unlike Great Britain, Ireland, India, Israel, and Pakistan, America has yet to see a woman head of state. In this activity, we will be learning about Woman's Suffrage and creating posters honoring all people's right to vote.

Materials

- composition paper
- 9" x 12" newsprint paper
- 12" x 18" posterboard (railroad board)
- 9" x 12" construction paper of assorted colors
- pencils
- markers
- rulers
- scissors
- white glue

Activity

1. Begin this activity by discussing what "voting" means. Why it is an important right in our country?

2. Ask the students why voting can make a difference. What would happen if people didn't vote? Why is choice a significant thing in a free country such as America? How many of their families vote?

28

3. Explain that many people in our country were originally denied the right to vote. African-Americans and women are but two examples. Hold a discussion that touches on the topics of slavery and woman's suffrage.

4. Explain that we will be creating posters that commemorate the right to vote. Distribute composition paper and ask each child to write a short slogan or message on voting. Examples might include "Don't Forget to Vote!" "Voting Gives You a Voice!", and the like.

5. Once the children have prepared their slogans, distribute the 9" x 12" newsprint paper, and ask them to make a simple illustration or design and include their slogan. Remind them that effective posters are simple and direct.

6. When the basic designs are completed, ask the children to transfer them to the 12" x 18" poster board using pencils and rulers. Slogan letters can be made even by using light pencil guidelines that can then be erased when the posters are completed.

7. Have students decorate and color their posters using markers, construction paper of assorted colors, white glue, and scissors.

8. When everyone has finished their work, hold a poster display and discussion.

Follow-Up

Construct a simple voting booth and hold a class election. Contact the League of Women Voters, and invite a speaker to address your class about voting. You might also consider asking the students to research the history of Susan B. Anthony and stage a reenactment of her historic battle for women's voting rights.

Helpful Books

- Ash, Maureen. *The Story of the Women's Movement.* Chicago: Childrens Press, 1989.
- Ingraham, Claire R. and Leonard W. *An Album of Women in American History.* New York: Franklin Watts, 1972.
- Kulkin, Mary-Ellen. *Her Way: Biographies of Women for Young People.* Chicago: American Library Association, 1976.
- Warren, Ruth. *A Pictorial History of Women in America.* New York: Crown Publishers, 1975.

WOMEN IN "HER" STORY

While most of us know about men in "his"story, all of us could probably benefit from learning more about women in "her"story. Gazing back into the past, we see that the role of women usually revolved around motherhood and family. These vocations are, of course, very important. Yet many women went beyond them to make other contributions to their world. These individuals often get little or no notice or attention for their efforts, which is why this activity is dedicated to them.

Before introducing the activity, it's a good idea to visit your local library to do some preliminary research. Next, compile a list of some of the unsung heroines. In the United States, the early history of our country is a good place to start. Anne Hutchinson, Deborah Sampson, Phillis Wheatley, Sacajawea, Sojourner Truth, Harriet Tubman, and many more contributed to the unique story of our land.

Materials

- 9" x 12" white drawing paper
- crayons
- pencils

Activity

1. Start the activity by holding a discussion about some of these remarkable women. Describe when they lived and what they did.

2. Ask each child to select one of these people and make a crayon drawing of her contribution.

3. When the selection process is complete, distribute the art materials and let the children get to work. Encourage them to

30

From *Celebrating Diversity with Art: Thematic Projects for Every Month of the Year,* published by GoodYearBooks. Copyright © 1995 by Willet Ryder.

work carefully on their drawings, and to write the name of their chosen person on the front of the drawing.

4. When the drawings are complete, hold a discussion session and art exhibit.

Follow-Up

Encourage the children to further investigate the women they chose, by doing some research in the classroom or school library. Ask each student to write a short composition on the person he/she selected and read it to the class.

Helpful Books

- Ingraham, Claire R. and Leonard W. *An Album of Women in American History.* New York: Franklin Watts, 1972.
- Kulkin, Mary-Ellen. *Her Way—Biographies of Women for Young People.* Chicago: American Library Association, 1976.
- Saxby, Maurice. *The Great Deeds of Heroic Women.* New York: Peter Bedrick Books, 1990.
- Warren, Ruth. *A Pictorial History of Women in America.* New York: Crown Publishers, 1975.

WOMEN IN THE ARTS AND SCIENCES

Marian Anderson, Elizabeth Blackwell, Mary Cassatt, Tiffany Chin, Marie Curie, Catherine D' Medici, Elma Gonzalez, Ru Chih Cheo Huang, Sophia Loren, Margaret Mead, Georgia O'Keefe, Sally Ride, Maria Tallchief, and Nancy Wallace—belong to a long list of notable women in the arts and sciences. Whether in the fields of anthropology, ballet, medicine, music or painting, women have established an amazing record of achievements. Their innumerable contributions span time and geography, and help to build a better, more creative world. The goal of this activity, is to develop children's awareness of the role of women in the arts and sciences. Before starting the activity, you may wish to do your own research on women in these fields. Head for your local library and compile some material on noteworthy women, perhaps making up a list of individual women and their contributions.

Materials

- 9" x 12" construction paper of assorted colors
- assorted construction paper scraps
- white glue
- scissors

Activity

1. Begin this activity by listing some names on the chalkboard and asking the children to identify them. Briefly discuss the contributions of a few individuals of your choice.

2. Next, provide the students with some research materials or a list of famous women and their accomplishments.

3. Ask each child to select one individual, about whom they will be making a cut paper design. Explain that the design can focus on either the person or the accomplishment. It can be done in any style from realistic to abstract.

4. After everyone has selected an individual, distribute the materials and let the work begin. When the designs are complete, ask each child to carefully letter on the front of the paper the name of the woman and her contribution.

5. Hold a sharing session and display of these art works.

Follow-Up

Invite a woman artist, dancer, dentist, doctor, musician, or scientist to speak to your class about her work.

Helpful Books

- Ash, Maureen. *The Story of the Women's Movement.* Chicago: Childrens Press, 1989.
- Collins, Jean E. *She Was There—Stories of Pioneering Women Journalists.* New York: Julian Messner, 1980.
- Ingraham, Claire R. and Leonard W. *An Album of Women in American History.* New York: Franklin Watts, 1972.
- Kulkin, Mary-Ellen. *Her Way—Biographies of Women for Young People.* Chicago: American Library Association, 1976.
- Warren, Ruth. *A Pictorial History of Women in America.* New York: Crown Publishers, 1975.

From *Celebrating Diversity with Art: Thematic Projects for Every Month of the Year,* published by GoodYearBooks. Copyright © 1995 by Willet Ryder.

WOMEN IN PUBLIC SERVICE

Hillary Rodham Clinton, Eleanor Roosevelt, Mother Teresa, Margaret Thatcher, Anne Hutchinson, Rosa Parks, Indira Ghandi and Golda Meir—these are but a few of the many names of women in public service. In this activity, we will investigate some of the individuals who have richly contributed to the public good. Unfortunately, children, and even adults, often have limited knowledge of women's endeavors in this area; indeed, they may be more aware of the contributions of men. This activity is devoted to uncovering the role of women in public service. Such a study will not only bolster girls' self-esteem and enlarge their sense of career opportunities, but will, hopefully, sensitize boys to the issue.

In preparing for this activity, you may want to conduct your own investigation. Take a trip to the school and local libraries and see what you can discover. Gather some books, posters, or pictures of famous women in public service. Look for some common themes: Note, for example, that many women have championed the causes of human rights and health. Next, formulate your own list of women and their contributions. After you have assembled this material, you're ready to begin.

Materials

- 9" x 12" newsprint
- 9" x 12" white drawing paper
- newspaper
- pencils
- crayons
- watercolors
- brushes
- water cups
- water
- paper towels

34

1. Bring the books and other materials you have collected to class, and launch a discussion about women in public service. You might put a group of names on the chalkboard and ask students if they can identify them. You could also discuss the meaning of "public service."

2. Distribute the list you assembled of women and their contributions, and briefly review it with your students.

3. Next, ask each child to select from the list one person/contribution (for example, Harriet Tubman and The Underground Railroad) to be the subject of a painting.

4. After the children have chosen an individual and topic, ask them to make a sketch using the newsprint paper and pencils. If they need to find out more information about the person, encourage them to look through your reference material or use the school library.

5. When the sketches are complete, distribute the other materials, and have the children transfer their sketches to the white drawing paper and make watercolor paintings. To create a "crayon resist," do the drawing first in crayon, and then paint over it in watercolor.

6. When the artwork has been completed, hold a sharing session and exhibit.

Follow-Up

Invite the children to further investigate the person they selected. Have them visit the library and do some research on this individual. Then, ask them to write a composition about the individual. This can serve as an accompaniment to the artwork on display.

Helpful Books

- Ash, Maureen. *The Story of the Women's Movement.* Chicago: Childrens Press, 1989.
- Biddle, Marcia McKenna. *Contributions of Women—Labor.* Minneapolis, MN: Dillon Press, 1979.
- Bowman, Kathleen. *New Women in Politics.* Mankato, MN: Creative Educational Society, 1976.
- Warren, Ruth. *A Pictorial History of Women in America.* New York: Crown Publishers, 1975.

QUILT PATCHES AND QUILTING

When I was a youth, my family had an old quilt that a distant relative had made. It not only kept us warm on a cold night, but also contained some fantastic patterns, colors and textures. The quilt no doubt included fabric remnants from clothing worn many years ago. Quilts are creations of great economy and imagination. They enabled people to carefully save and utilize every scrap, rather than throwing it out. Besides being utilitarian objects, quilts provided their makers with a creative outlet for needle, thread, and cloth. Quilting generally fell to the women, since women were, for the most part, in charge of making clothes and keeping them in good repair. Quilting bees, occasions on which women gathered to work collectively on quilts, provided opportunities for sharing both fabric and information. With the renewed popularity today of quilts, quilting groups are also on the rise. Many contemporary artists, such as Faith Ringgold and Remare Bearden, use quilting to tell stories and awaken social awareness. The AIDS Quilt, too, serves as a special memorial to those who have died from the disease.

In this activity, we will be using construction paper of assorted colors and scraps of cloth to design our own quilt patches. Several weeks before starting the activity, ask the children to begin bringing in scraps of old material.

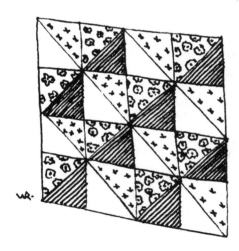 

Materials

- 9" x 12" construction paper of assorted colors
- fabric scraps
- scissors
- white glue

36

Activity

1. If you have a homemade quilt at home or if you are a quilter, bring in a quilt or quilt section to show the class. If you don't have an actual quilt, bring in some pictures or books about quilting to share with the children.

2. Discuss why quilting was important in the history of our country and why it is becoming popular today.

3. Next, briefly explain how a quilt patch is made—using bits of cloth to create a design, which is then sewn together. Is it possible to be creative with bits of scrap material?

4. Then, have children select an assortment of construction paper and cloth scraps. Ask them to carefully study their selections and begin arranging the materials in a rough design.

5. Distribute the scissors and glue, and let the children begin cutting and pasting together their designs. Remind students that because fabric is porous, it will take a while for the glue to harden.

6. Let the patches dry thoroughly, and then hold a quilt patch discussion and display.

Follow-Up

Find out if your community has a group of quilters. Invite members of the group to show their quilts and discuss their interest in quilting with the class.

Helpful Books

- Johnston, Tony. *The Quilt Story.* New York: Putnam's, 1985.
- Paul, Ann Whitford. *Eight Hands Round: A Patchwork Alphabet.* New York: HarperCollinsPublishers, 1991.
- Ratner, Marilyn. *Plenty of Patches.* New York: Thomas Y. Crowell, 1978.
- Ringgold, Faith. *Aunt Harriet's Underground Road in the Sky.* New York: Scholastic Inc., 1992.
- Ringgold, Faith. *Tar Beach.* New York: Scholastic Inc., 1991.

LIBERTY: A FAMOUS STATUE

A giant woman stands on a small island in New York Harbor. She is made of bronze and was given as a gift, in 1886, to the United States by France. Sculpted by Auguste Bartholdi, the one-of-a-kind statue contains a series of steps built into her core, enabling people to climb to the crown and torch. As one gazes at this amazing sculpture, it is impossible not to be struck by the look of her special strength, determination, and compassion. Lady Liberty holds a tablet in the crook of one arm and carries a lighted torch, held high, in her other hand. Inscribed at her base is the famous poem written by another famous woman, Emma Lazarus, that has welcomed countless immigrants to these shores. In this activity, we will be focusing on the Statue of Liberty and creating unique drawings of this historical landmark.

Materials

- 12" x 18" newsprint and white drawing paper
- pencils
- crayons
- markers

Activity

1. Begin the activity by showing pictures of the statue. Hold a short discussion in which you explain a little of its history.

2. Ask the children to pay close attention to the details of the statue. What is she carrying? What kind of crown is she wearing? What is inscribed on the tablet she is holding?

38

3. Next, distribute the newsprint paper and pencils, and ask each child to make an imaginative sketch or two of his/her rendition of this famous statue. Spend some time discussing various artistic styles—whether abstract, realistic, impressionist, etc.—and remind students that the style they choose is up to them. Encourage them to be original!

4. When the sketches are complete, have each student select his/her favorite and transfer it to white drawing paper. Children can color the drawings using the crayons and markers. Here again, encourage the children to be creative in their choice of colors and designs. Perhaps someone will draw a Statue of Liberty with a red robe and a neon torch, or one with a floral print gown and carrying a large flashlight. Humor and whimsy should be stressed!

5. When the drawings are complete, hold a discussion and exhibit.

Follow-Up

Read the poem by Emma Lazarus, and ask the children to write an essay or poem about what "liberty" means to them. The class can hold a special reading to go along with the Liberty art exhibit. Perhaps some of the children have relatives who passed by the Statue of Liberty en route to America from a distant land. Ask them to interview their relatives and write—up their stories to share with the class. If you are lucky enough to live near New York, take a trip to visit this wonderful statue. You might also pay a visit to the fine museum at Ellis Island.

Helpful Books

- Fisher, Leonard Everett. *The Statue of Liberty.* New York: Holiday House, 1985.
- Handlin, Oscar. *Statue of Liberty.* New York: Newsweek Book Division, 1971.
- Hargrove, Jim. *Gateway to Freedom.* Chicago: Childrens Press, 1986.
- Maestro, Betsy and Giulio. *The Story of the Statue of Liberty.* New York: Lothrop, Lee & Shepard, 1986.

39

Keeping our country beautiful can be accomplished on at least two broad levels. We can focus our attention on maintaining the natural beauty of our physical environment or we can work to improve the human condition—that is, our human environment. Sometimes the two missions overlap! Problems of waste and pollution threaten our physical environment. Empty cans, bits of paper, broken bottles, old cartons, plastic containers, and chemical liquids and vapors foul our water, air and land. For that matter, they menace our entire planet. There is no question that more efficient recycling and better environmental clean-up procedures can make for more beautiful surroundings, and, hopefully, happier people. Similarly problems of loneliness, homelessness, poverty, and despair threaten our human environment. Think, for example, of those who live in nursing homes, orphanages, or temporary shelters. For these individuals, the caring concern of others may go a long way to bolster their spirits. In both these scenarios, all of us, including our school children, can improve the quality of American life by getting involved! The activities for this month are dedicated to doing just that—they include a variety of experiences designed to keep America beautiful.

A LOCAL COMMUNITY PROJECT

You and your class can do something wonderful to link school and neighborhood in a special partnership, and teach kids about community responsibility. You can launch or join a special project designed to help improve your local area. You might plant some trees or flowers on the school grounds, paint a mural on the empty wall of a building, help decorate a store window, sing songs at a nursing home, or make small gifts for residents of a halfway house. Every community has a-thousand-and-one needs, and schools can really lend a helping hand. This activity challenges each of us to carefully consider our communities and find ways to make them more attractive and comfortable for all.

Materials

- It depends on your particular project

Activity

1. Begin this activity by carefully evaluating your local community and noting what needs to be done. Keep your eyes and ears open! Talk to people in the area, and listen to their comments. Look around the neighborhood and pick out things that need work. After you have selected a project, make sure that you obtain approval from your school principal.

2. Next, introduce your students to the project. You may wish to relate a story or show them photos or slides of what you have in

From *Celebrating Diversity with Art: Thematic Projects for Every Month of the Year*, published by GoodYearBooks. Copyright © 1995 by Willet Ryder.

mind. Explain that the aim will be to make things more attractive and help make people happier.

3. Once you've discussed the project with the children, be sure to send information home to the parents or guardians. It is crucial that all parents and guardians give permission for their children to be involved!

4. Once you begin, try to document your class's involvement by taking lots of photos or videotaping segments of your activity. You may also wish to write a short article and submit it, along with some photos, to the local newspaper.

Follow-Up

Remember that organizing or taking part in a community project takes time and commitment. It may, in fact, be an ongoing activity which extends for some or all of the school year. Children can gain invaluable experience by helping others in their community and making their world a brighter place! This activity was inspired by my wife, Eleanor Ryder, who regularly involves her fourth-grade class in community projects. Her class activities have included: singing songs to nursing home residents, holding a crafts fair to raise money for needy families within the community, raising money for a local orphanage, and planting trees to beautify the environment.

Helpful Books

- Bramwell, Martyn. *The Environment and Conservation.* New York: Prentice-Hall, 1992.
- Markle, Sandra. *The Kids' Earth Handbook.* New York: Atheneum, 1991.
- Wilson, Marlene. *You Can Make A Difference!* Boulder, CO: Volunteer Management Associates, 1990.

From *Celebrating Diversity with Art: Thematic Projects for Every Month of the Year,* published by GoodYearBooks. Copyright © 1995 by Willet Ryder.

ECOLOGY POSTERS

"Save the Whales," "Don't be a Litterbug," "Protect our Forests"—these are but a few slogans that spring to mind when one considers the goals of ecology. The United States has many important issues to address with regard to ecology and conservation. These include protecting animals and natural resources; developing awareness of the perils of water, soil, and air pollution; and, of course, preserving the welfare and safety of human beings.

Before introducing this activity, take a moment to carefully consider the topic of ecology and to identify a few areas about which you are especially concerned. Remember that many ecological issues are controversial and could lead to lively debate. Protecting certain owl species, for example, is fine for our feathered friends, but may negatively impact the lumberjack whose job it is to cut down the tree (the owls' home) in order to make a living.

Materials

- 9" x 12" newsprint paper
- 12" x 18" construction paper of assorted colors
- 12" x 18" poster board of assorted colors
- pencils
- markers
- crayons
- rulers
- scissors
- white glue

Activity

1. Introduce the concept of ecology by asking your class some questions. What is ecology? Why is it important for us? Perhaps tell the children about a few of your ecological concerns.

2. Ask the children to think about some of their ecological concerns, and make a list of these on the chalkboard, as they answer.

From *Celebrating Diversity with Art: Thematic Projects for Every Month of the Year,* published by GoodYearBooks. Copyright © 1995 by Willet Ryder.

3. When you have compiled a long list, ask each child to select one issue that interests him/her the most. Then distribute the 9" x 12" newsprint paper and pencils, and invite the children to sketch some ideas for an ecology poster.

4. Once these are done, have each child select her/his favorite sketch and transfer it to the 12" x 18" posterboard. Encourage the children to cut their designs out of construction paper and glue these to the posterboard, rather than use crayons and markers to draw on it. (Cut-paper designs tend to stand out more and are crisper-looking than crayon and marker.) Letters can also be cut from the construction paper. Reserve markers and crayons for embellishing the cut paper designs and doing the lettering as needed.

5. Regarding the poster slogans, remind children to keep the wording short and simple. They should use the pencils and rulers to draw guidelines for themselves before doing the lettering with markers or crayons.

6. When the posters are complete, hold a sharing session and display the posters in the school hallway.

Follow-Up

Invite a speaker to address the class about an ecological issue. If you happen to live near a national park, you may be able to find a speaker through the U.S. Park Service. Ask the children to write compositions about the issues they address in their posters, explaining their importance in more detail.

Helpful Books

- Bramwell, Martyn. *The Environment and Conservation.* New York: Prentice-Hall, 1992.
- Doubilet, Anne. *Under the Sea from A to Z.* New York: Crown Publishers, 1991.
- Jorgenson, Lisa. *Grand Trees of America.* Niwot, CO: Roberts Rinehart Publishers, 1992.
- National Wildlife Federation. *Incredible Animals A to Z.* Washington, DC: National Wildlife Federation, 1985.
- Seattle, Chief. *Brother Eagle, Sister Sky.* New York: Dial Books, 1991.

SCULPTURE FROM RECYCLABLE MATERIALS

Styrofoam, cardboard, bottle caps,
and fancy wraps.

Ribbons, strings, buttons, bows.
Lots of stuff before your nose.

Just look around your house or yard.
You'll find things—It's not that hard!

Our world is full of all kinds of recyclable materials. All we have to do is look! Ask your students to start bringing in such materials a week or so before beginning this activity. Don't forget to add your own recyclables to the class collection. Once the children have accumulated a bunch of things, you're ready to start.

Materials

- a variety of recyclable materials
- construction paper of assorted colors and paper scraps
- toothpicks
- pencils
- markers
- scissors
- white glue

Activity

1. Hold a brief discussion about recyclable items. What are they? What can we do with them?

2. Explain that we will be making sculptures from recyclable items. Before distributing any materials, remind everyone to experiment with the placement and design of these items before gluing them in place.

45

3. Next, distribute the materials and let the work begin. Students can use markers and construction paper of assorted colors to embellish their sculptures.

4. When the works are complete, hold a recyclable sculpture show in the classroom or hall showcase.

Follow-Up

Visit a recycling center, if one is located nearby your school. Invite an official from a conservation organization or recycling agency to speak to your class.

Helpful Books

- Bailey, Donna. *What We Can Do About Recycling Garbage.* New York: Franklin Watts, 1991.
- Carlson, Laurie. *EcoArt!* Charlotte, VT: Williamson Publishing, 1993.
- Carlson, Laurie. *Kids Create!* Charlotte, VT: Williamson Publishing, 1990.
- Gibbons, Gail. *Recycle! A Handbook for Kids.* Boston: Little, Brown, 1992.
- Gutnik, Martin J. *Experiments That Explore Recycling.* Brookfield, CT: The Millbrook Press, 1992.

From *Celebrating Diversity with Art: Thematic Projects for Every Month of the Year,* published by GoodYearBooks. Copyright © 1995 by Willet Ryder.

LEARNING TO SAVE OUR RESOURCES

Our natural resources—animals, plants, air, water, soil, and minerals—are valuable and vital. All of us need to understand that unless we carefully monitor and conserve these things now, the world of the future will be a very bleak place indeed. In our own country, many animals and plants have already become extinct, because of careless management and greed. The message is clear: We must do a better job of conserving our natural resources, or suffer the sad consequences. To help drive home that point, this activity asks each child to select a natural resource and create a watercolor painting about it.

Materials

- 9" x 12" manila paper
- 12" x 18" white drawing paper
- pencils
- watercolors
- brushes
- water
- water cups
- newspaper
- paper towels

Activity

1. Discuss the meaning of a "natural resource." Explain that our natural resources—things we all enjoy to be happy, healthy, and comfortable, need to be protected. Minerals, such as coal and oil, the air we breathe, the things we eat, the plants and animals around us, and the water we drink, are all part of our natural resources.

2. After this discussion, ask each student to select a natural resource that he/she feels strongly about. Explain that we will be making paintings about these resources, using any artistic style we would like. One child might paint a realistic picture of a factory polluting the air, for example, while another might do an abstract design of the same subject.

3. Distribute the manila paper and pencils, and ask each child to make a sketch of their idea.

4. When the sketches are complete, distribute the white drawing paper, and ask the children to transfer their sketches to the larger sheets using pencil.

5. Next, distribute the rest of the materials and let the class begin painting.

6. When the paintings are complete, hold a sharing session and exhibit.

Follow-Up

Invite each student to research and write a composition about the resource she/he selected. The school library should be a good source of information.

Helpful Books

- Bramwell, Martyn. *The Environment and Conservation.* New York: Prentice-Hall, 1992.

- Doubilet, Anne. *Under the Sea from A to Z.* New York: Crown Publishers, 1991.

- Jorgenson, Lisa. *Grand Trees of America.* Niwot, CO: Roberts Rinehart Publishers, 1992.

- Markham, Adam. *The Environment.* Vera Beach, FL: Rourke Enterprises, 1988.

- National Wildlife Federation. *Incredible Animals A to Z.* Washington, DC: National Wildlife Foundation, 1985.

From *Celebrating Diversity with Art: Thematic Projects for Every Month of the Year,* published by GoodYearBooks. Copyright © 1995 by Willet Ryder.

COLLECTING CANS

It's fun to redeem empty cans at the local supermarket, but you can also turn the cans into neat creatures. To make your own "can man" or "can woman," all you need is a clean empty juice or soda can, some simple materials, and a little imagination! Before starting this activity, hold a class or school drive to accumulate empty cans.

Materials

- clean, empty cans (juice or soda)
- 9" x 12" construction paper of assorted colors
- fluorescent paper
- markers
- scissors
- cellophane tape
- white glue
- assorted found objects

Activity

1. Begin this activity by showing a can creature that you have made at home. Point out that cans can be recycled or turned into fascinating creatures.

2. Before distributing the materials to the children, briefly explain the general procedure for making these creations:

   a. Take a clean, empty can and roll it tightly in a sheet of 9" x 12" construction or fluorescent paper. Make sure that one end of the can is flush with the edge of the paper. Apply some white glue to the end of the paper, and hold it fast by using a few pieces of cellophane tape.

   b. From construction or fluorescent paper, cut out feet with long tabs at the end. Put a little glue on the tabs and slide them

49

between the can and the paper covering at the front of the can. When the glue has set, bend the feet forward.

c. Add arms, eyes, nose, mouth, and ears by cutting them from the construction paper and gluing them to the covered can.

d. Great hair can be made by fringing the leftover paper at the top of the can. If you wish to cut this extra paper off, and add an imaginative hat, you can do so.

e. Extra decorations can be added by using markers and gluing on assorted found objects, such as buttons, feathers, spangles, etc.

3. Next, distribute the materials to the children and let the fun begin!

4. When the "can creatures" are finished, you "can" have a display!

Follow-Up

Turn in the extra cans from your class can drive, and donate the money to a good cause and/or hold a small class party.

Helpful Books

- Carlson, Laurie. *EcoArt!* Charlotte, VT: Williamson Publishing, 1993.
- Carlson, Laurie. *Kids Create!* Charlotte, VT: Williamson Publishing, 1990.
- Foster, Joanna. *Cartons, Cans, and Orange Peels: Where Does Your Garbage Go?* New York: Clarion Books, 1991.

INVENTORS' NIGHT

"Originality," "creativity," and "genius" are some terms that describe an inventor. There is little question, however, that an inventor also needs a sense of humor. I owe the idea of Inventors' Night to my wife, Eleanor Ryder, who organizes one each year for her fourth-grade class. In this activity, we will be building and presenting our own inventions. The point is to be creative to use found objects in an ingenious way. Whether the inventions function or not is less important than whether they inspire interest in the viewers.

Several weeks prior to starting this project, send a note home to the parents, asking them to begin collecting a variety of found objects in a shoebox for their children. Items can include bottle tops, cans, string, buttons, Styrofoam, and the like. Set a specific due date, and request that the shoeboxes containing these objects be sent to school by that time. Once all the shoeboxes have been received, you are ready to begin working with the class. Be sure to bring in a variety of extra materials from home in case someone has few found objects or doesn't have a shoebox at all.

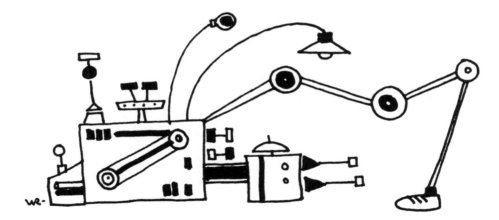

Materials

- found objects
- 9" x 12" newsprint paper
- pencils
- crayons
- markers
- construction paper of assorted colors and paper scraps
- white glue
- rulers
- scissors
- string and/or yarn

Activity

1. Begin this activity by discussing the idea of an "invention." How do inventors work?

2. Discuss some famous inventors, such as Benjamin Franklin, Elijah McCoy, and others.

51

3. Next, explain that each child will be creating an invention out of the objects found in his/her shoebox. Be sure to mention that inventors have to be ingenious in using materials.

4. Pass out the shoeboxes, and encourage each child to carefully consider the items she/he finds. How can they be put together? What do they remind you of? Ask the children to make sketches of their ideas on newsprint paper and to experiment with manipulating the various materials.

5. When each child has selected his/her best idea, it's time to glue the invention together and decorate it.

6. When all the inventions are completed, invite the children's parents to a special "Inventors' Night" so that parents can see and hear about their children's creations.

Follow-Up

Ask the children to write a short composition about their inventions.

Helpful Books

- Aaseng, Nathan. *Twentieth Century Inventors.* New York: Facts on File, 1991.
- Jones, Charlotte Foltz. *Mistakes That Worked.* New York: Doubleday, 1991.
- Weiss, Harvey. *How to Be an Inventor.* New York: Thomas Y. Crowell, 1980.

Asian-Pacific American Heritage Month

China, India, Fiji, Japan, Hawaii, and New Zealand—these are but a few of the places that spring to mind when one considers Asia and the Pacific. This vast area is filled to overflowing with adventure and mystery! From the craters of Halieikala in the state of Hawaii to the Great Wall of China, from the Taj Mahal in India to the Glowworm Caves of New Zealand, we are introduced to cultures and facts very different from those in the West. During Asian-Pacific Heritage month, we will investigate and learn about the people and philosophies from a fascinating part of our world. We will design tiki pendants and make drawings inspired by the music of the South Seas. We will find out what a tea ceremony is and learn how to use chopsticks. We will also celebrate an Indian festival and make decorative kites. So, put on your traveling clothes and get your knapsack ready—we're about to begin a new journey!

DESIGNING TIKI PENDANTS

Islands extend across the Pacific Ocean like a broken string of pearls. Some island groups, such as Hawaii, Fiji, and Tahiti, are composed of many smaller islands. Pacific Islanders made great trips from place to place. They carried their artistic symbols and concepts with them. One of these is the Tiki head, a guardian representing good luck and a protector against evil. Tiki are represented in large island sculptural works as well as in small personal jewelry. These smaller pieces are often carved from wood or jade, fastened to a cord or chain, and worn around the neck. In this activity, we will be designing and creating our own tiki pendants.

<table>
<tr><td>Materials</td><td>

- 9" x 12" newsprint paper
- 2" x 3" green posterboard
- 3" x 4" clear Contact paper

</td><td>

- pencils
- fine-tipped markers
- yarn
- scissors
- hole punches

</td></tr>
</table>

Activity

1. Begin this activity by showing children the Pacific area and pointing out some of the island groups. Ask the children if they, or their relatives, are from any of these islands or have visited them. Remember to remind the children that Hawaii is part of the United States. Explain that Pacific Islanders make sculptures and jewelry of faces which they believe help to bring protection and good luck.

2. Next, show some pictures of tiki sculpture or jewelry, and discuss some of the designs. Ask the children to comment on what they notice in these examples. Point out that each face is slightly different.

3. Explain that we will be designing and creating our own tiki pendants. Distribute the newsprint paper and pencils, and ask each child to make a group of sketches for his/her pendant.

4. Then distribute the 2" x 3" green posterboard, and ask each child to select his/her favorite face design and transfer it to the posterboard, using light pencil lines.

5. Once the sketches have been transferred, children can darken and color them using fine-tipped markers.

6. After the posterboard designs are completed, distribute the 3" x 4" pieces of clear Contact paper. Ask each child to peel the protective backing off the paper and carefully affix the clear paper over the front of his/her pendant.

7. Next, pass out the scissors, and ask the children to trim off the excess Contact paper. Small triangular cuts can also be made at the edge of the pendants to enhance the designs.

8. Next, use the hole punch to make a hole in the top center of each pendant. To simplify this process, you, as the teacher, may wish to be the official hole puncher!

9. Distribute long pieces of pre-cut yarn (2 to 3 feet). Have the children string their pendant and tie the ends so that it can be slipped over the head.

Follow-Up

Hold a tiki pendant display in the school showcase, along with a map of some Pacific island groups. Organize a tiki pendant sale and use the money to adopt a whale at your local aquarium or have a class luau.

Helpful Books

- Price, Christine. *Made in the South Pacific.* New York: Dutton, 1979.

DRAWING TO ISLAND MUSIC

Many years ago, while visiting my wife's homeland, New Zealand, we spent a wonderful evening in Rotorua, listening to a group of Maori singers. The marvelous sounds of their songs made the listener aware not only of beautiful vocal harmonies, but conjured up special images of the Pacific Islands. Hawaiian music does much the same thing! Island music make me think of long, starlit sea voyages by outrigger canoe or palm trees swaying near the edge of a desolate beach. What images do they conjure up for you?

In this activity, we will listen carefully to some music from the Pacific Islands, and attempt to draw our impressions in visual form. Before starting the activity, spend a little time locating a good cassette, record, or CD of music of the Pacific Islands. Many local libraries carry such selections. After you have made your choice, listen to it several times before playing it for your class. Make your own drawing or design, and jot down a short list of things you noticed about the music.

Materials

- a cassette tape, record, or CD of Pacific Island music (for example, from Hawaii, Tahiti, Fiji, or New Zealand)
- tape recorder, or record or CD player
- 9" x 12" white drawing paper
- markers or crayons in assorted colors

Activity

1. Begin the activity by explaining to the class that we will be listening and drawing to music from the Pacific Islands. Briefly discuss the location of some of these islands, pointing them out on a world map.

2. Explain to the children that the drawings or designs do not have to be realistic. They can be abstract shapes and lines, dashes and dots, or squiggles of colors. The important thing is to listen carefully to the music and really think about the impressions it gives to you! Be sure to tell the children not to begin drawing until the music starts.

3. Next, distribute the paper, markers, and crayons. Then turn on the music and let the activity begin. You may wish to walk about the room as the students work, or do your own drawing.

4. When the designs are complete, hold a discussion and sharing session about this activity.

5. Mount the drawings on construction paper of assorted colors and exhibit them in the hallway or classroom.

Follow-Up

Bring in an island fruit, such as a kiwi or passion fruit, and let the children sample it while listening to the tape. Discuss their impressions of its taste.

Helpful Books

- Ball, John and Fairclough, Chris. *Let's Visit Fiji.* London: Burke Publishing Company Limited, 1985.
- Ford, Douglas. *The Pacific Islanders.* New York: Chelsea House Publishers, 1989.
- McNair, Sylvia. *Hawaii—America the Beautiful.* Chicago: Childrens Press, 1990.

THE TEA CEREMONY

Tea is a very popular drink in the East and is, in fact, the focus of a special ceremony in Japan. A true tea ceremony is not only about tea. It is also about the entire process of preparing, serving, and enjoying this drink in special surroundings. The idea of becoming totally involved in enjoying a cup of tea, having a meal, making a painting, or contemplating a scene is related to the philosophy of Zen Buddhism. This philosophy encourages individuals to become fully involved in whatever they are pursuing, to the exclusion of other things. In doing so, they come to truly enjoy and appreciate any activity.

Materials

- an earthenware cup
- a package of plastic cups
- napkins
- a thermos of iced herbal tea
- a simple vase with a floral arrangement
- a print or photo of a natural scene
- cassette tape recorder
- a tape of Japanese koto (zither) music
- 9" x 12" newsprint paper
- pencils
- watercolors
- water
- water cups
- brushes
- paper towels

Activity

1. Arrange the print or photo you have selected in the front of the room. Set up the vase with flowers nearby, and put on the koto music.

2. Next, introduce the tea ceremony, and explain its importance in the Far East. Point out the objects in the front of the room and briefly discuss them.

58

3. Then, pass around the simple ceramic cup, and let each child look at it and feel its texture.

4. Explain to the children that you will soon be distributing cups of herbal iced tea. Next, distribute the tea, and let the children enjoy its flavor while listening to the music.

5. After collecting the empty cups, ask each child to think about creating a painting inspired by the tea ceremony. Then, pass out the art materials, and let the work commence.

6. When the paintings are complete, hold a sharing session and exhibit.

Follow-Up

Take a class trip to a Japanese or Chinese restaurant, and enjoy a meal together.

Helpful Books

- Bartok, Mira, and Ronan, Christine. *Ancient and Living Cultures: Ancient Japan.* Glenview, IL: GoodYearBooks, 1993.
- Downer, Lesley. *Japan.* New York: The Bookwright Press, 1990.
- Tanaka, Seno. *The Tea Ceremony.* Tokyo: Kodansha International Ltd., 1973.

59

USING CHOPSTICKS

Chopsticks are joyful utensils with which to eat, and they're lots of fun when it comes to creating artworks. This activity, which draws on both uses, requires a good supply of chopsticks. You can obtain chopsticks by contacting a local Asian restaurant or restaurant supply house. If you live in or near the Chinese section of a large city, you'll find many shops and groceries stock chopsticks. For this activity, the chopsticks should be simple, without any surface decorations. I prefer the flat wooden variety, which you have to snap into two sticks before using. Try to purchase chopsticks that have a "how to use them" diagram printed on the cover. This will come in handy later! In this activity, we will be using chopsticks for both eating and creating! If you're not sure about how to use them, visit a Chinese restaurant or cook a few Chinese meals and practice.

Materials

- chopsticks (1 pair per student)
- paper bowls
- cut fruit, such as oranges
- napkins
- plasticine
- movable plastic eyes (smallest size)
- feathers
- construction paper scraps of assorted colors
- yarn
- fine-tipped markers
- white glue
- scissors

Activity

1. Begin this activity by noting that people in various parts of the world eat differently. In parts of Asia, such as China, Japan, and Southeast Asia, people use chopsticks instead of knives and forks.

2. Ask how many children have used chopsticks. If someone in your class can use them, ask him/her to help you show students their use. Briefly demonstrate how chopsticks work, and refer the children to the diagram printed on each package.

3. Next, distribute a pair of chopsticks to each child, along with a small bowl of fruit and a napkin. Give the kids some time to experiment with the chopsticks, and move about the room to help them.

4. When the fruit has been devoured, throw away the paper bowls and napkins, and explain that we will be making "stick people" with our chopsticks. These can be made by selecting a chopstick, decorating it by adding eyes, hair, paper limbs, and clothes, and then pressing the base of the stick into a lump of plasticine.

5. At this point, you may wish to show the class some "stick people" that you have created at home. Distribute the necessary materials, and let the fun begin. Remember to caution the children that very little glue is needed in this activity.

6. When the "stick people" are finished, hold a discussion and setup a display in the school show case.

Follow-Up

Plan a simple Chinese meal and invite children's parents and grandparents to attend. Let the children teach their relatives how to use chopsticks!

Helpful Books

- Ashley, Bernard. *Cleversticks.* New York: Crown Publishers, 1991.
- San, Hashi. *Chopsticks! An Owner's Manual.* Berkeley, CA: Conari Press, 1991.

INDIAN FESTIVAL

India is a land of tremendous diversity and many beliefs. Although the majority of its residents are Hindu, India is also home to Buddhists, Sikhs, Muslims, Jainists, and Zoroastrians. A great variety of festivals take place throughout the year. Since it is impossible to consider them all, I have selected the Hindu festival of Divali. Although Divali is usually held in the autumn, we will be celebrating it during the spring. Divali is a festival of lamps and light, when Hindu families welcome Lakshmi, the goddess of good fortune and wealth, into their home and hope for a prosperous year ahead. Given the major emphasis of the holiday on lamps and lights, we will be designing our own fancy lamps to commemorate this festival.

Materials

- 9" x 12" newsprint paper
- 9" x 12" and 12" x 18" construction paper of assorted colors
- gold and silver foil
- pencils
- markers
- scissors
- white glue

Activity

1. Hold a discussion on Divali and/or read a story about this Indian holiday. Show where India is located on the map, and talk a bit about this fascinating country.

2. Explain the importance of lamps and lighting for this holiday, and ask the children to design their own festival lamp. remind students that such lamps do not have to be electric, but can be oil-burning, like "Aladdin's lamp."

3. Distribute the newsprint paper and pencils, and ask each child to make some sketches of his/her lamp.

4. Next, ask each child to select his/her favorite design, and create a lamp using the construction paper, foil, markers, glue, and scissors.

5. Hold a discussion and exhibition at the conclusion of the activity.

Follow-Up

Read some books about Divali and other Indian festivals. Ask the children to do brief oral reports about selected Indian holidays.

Helpful Books

- Asian Copublication Programme. *Festivals in Asia.* Tokyo: Kodansha International Ltd., 1975.
- Bond, Ruskin. *Cherry Tree.* Honesdale, PA: Caroline House, 1991.
- McNair, Sylvia. *India.* Chicago: Childrens Press, 1990.
- Watson, Jane Werner. *India Celebrates!* Champaign, IL: Garrard Publishing Company, 1974.

MAKING DECORATIVE KITES

Kites are marvelous things, and are designed and flown in many parts of the world. In sections of Asia, kites often take on a special creative twist. Some kites depict insects, birds, and other animals. Other kites are based on mythical creatures, such as dragons. Some Chinese and Japanese kites appear to be too beautiful to fly! In this activity, we will be designing and creating our own decorative kites. These kites will be used for looking, rather than for flying.

Materials

- 9" x 12" newsprint paper
- 12" x 18" construction paper of assorted colors
- tissue paper
- crepe paper
- construction paper scraps
- yarn
- white glue
- pencils
- markers
- scissors
- hole punches

Activity

1. Begin the activity by discussing kites and kite flying. Ask the children how many of them have ever flown a kite.

2. Explain that we will be making decorative kites, not flying kites, based on themes taken from nature or from your imagination.

3. Ask the children to help compile a list of possible kite themes, and write these on the chalkboard. Examples might include dragons, fish, butterflies, birds, flowers, and the like.

64

4. Distribute the 9" x 12" newsprint paper and pencils, and invite each child to sketch some designs for her/his own kite.

5. After the children have come up with a few designs, ask them to select their favorite. Each should then transfer his/her design to the 12" x 18" sheets of construction paper. If the kite design is symmetrical, remind students that they can cut out the kite shape by folding the paper and cutting only half the design.

6. Have students decorate the kites using the paper scraps, tissue paper, markers, scissors, and white glue.

7. When the kites are complete, make a small hole in each kite with the hole punch, and attach some yarn for exhibiting. Fancy tails can be added by using the rolled crepe paper.

8. Hold a kite sharing session and exhibit.

Follow-Up

Read some stories about kites. Purchase a few flying kites that you and your students can fly in the school yard, if space permits.

Helpful Books

- Gibbons, Gail. *Catch the Wind!* Boston: Little, Brown, 1989.
- Greger, Margaret. *Blown Sky-High—A Book of Kites.* Richland, WA: Locust Grove Press, 1977.
- Newman, Lee Scott, and Newman, Jay Hartley. *Kite Craft.* New York: Crown Publishers, 1974.
- Ryder, Willet. *The Art Experience.* Glenview, IL: GoodYearBooks, 1991.

Zoo
And
Aquarium
Month

Prairie dogs are pretty curious animals! I know, because on a recent trip to the Bronx Zoo with my wife's fourth grade class, I was able to study their behavior in a fascinating section of the Children's Zoo. The section features a special hill containing several prairie dog burrows, along with a number of separate tunnels and plexiglass viewing tubes designed for children. So, as a few children would appear in their special tubes, protected by plexiglass, the prairie dogs would surface and peer out of their own burrows to watch the kids. What a humorous thing it was to see kids and prairie dogs popping in and out of burrows to look at one another!

Zoos and conservation parks are great fun and provide us with a wealth of information. In a day and age when people are much more aware than they used to be of animal rights, most zoos have abandoned the restrictive cages and steel bars of the past, and created larger and freer environments that reflect the animals' natural habitats. In one section of the Bronx Zoo, a giant structure has been erected to house a miniature version of a tropical rain forest. Water cascades from cliffs, and trees and moss abound. Crocodiles patrol the moving streams, while monkeys chatter in the treetops and birds dart about. From overhanging rocks, water drips down on the visitors below as they follow the trail through this wonderful, wet world.

During the month of June, we all have a wonderful opportunity to pay homage to zoos and aquariums by celebrating Zoo and Aquarium Month. For without places like the Bronx Zoo and SeaWorld, many of us might never see some of the marvelous co-inhabitants of our planet. This section of the book contains a number of exciting creative activities that celebrate these special institutions.

From *Celebrating Diversity with Art: Thematic Projects for Every Month of the Year,* published by GoodYearBooks. Copyright © 1995 by Willet Ryder.

CRAZY CROCS

Probably the most famous crocodile of all appears in the play Peter Pan. This animal is so mean that he can even throw fear into the evil Captain Hook! In this activity, we will be learning about crocodiles and other reptiles, such as alligators, lizards, snakes, and turtles. Although reptiles scare some people, children seem to be especially fascinated by these interesting creatures.

Materials

- 9" x 12" construction paper of assorted colors and paper scraps
- pencils
- crayons
- markers
- white glue
- cellophane tape
- scissors

Activity

1. To start this activity, have the children go to the school library and do some research on reptiles. Ask each child to write down a few facts about the reptile of her/his choice. Remind children to include such information as where these animals live, what they eat, and the like.

2. Next, hold a discussion about reptiles, and show the class a "Crazy Croc" that you have made at home (see instructions below). Explain that this fantasy animal can be decorated and individualized in many different ways.

3. You can create a "Crazy Croc" by following these steps:

   a. Roll a sheet of construction paper into a cone, by starting at one corner. Tape or glue the end, after you finish rolling it, so that it doesn't come loose. Even out the wide end by trimming it with your scissors.

67

From *Celebrating Diversity with Art: Thematic Projects for Every Month of the Year,* published by GoodYearBooks. Copyright © 1995 by Willet Ryder.

b. Fold a second sheet of paper, using either the same or a different color, and cut a head in the following way:

c. Next, cut a small rectangle of paper, fold it in the following fashion and draw some eyes on the top.

Glue this rectangle to the top of the croc's head, and attach the head to the wide end of the cone.

d. Fold a rectangle of paper twice, and cut an interesting foot design. Attach the two pairs of feet to the bottom of the cone.

e. Finally, decorate the "Crazy Croc" using an imaginative approach! Crayons, markers, assorted color scraps of construction paper, glue, and scissors can be used for this purpose.

Follow-Up

Create a display of the crocs in the classroom or school library. You might use a table, window ledge, or library shelf for this purpose. Don't forget to add plants and rocks to enhance the scene! Most high school biology classes have some reptiles in their collections. Why not arrange a trip to your local high school to visit the reptiles and hear a talk by a high school teacher or her/his students. A trip to a nearby zoo or conservation park to see the reptile collection is always a great experience. Needless to say, if some of the children have reptile pets, you might arrange for them to bring these to school for a show-and-tell session.

Helpful Books

- Cloudsley-Thompson, John. *Crocodiles & Alligators*. East Sussex, England: Wayland Limited, 1984.
- Frank, Werner. *Boas and Other Non-Venomous Snakes*. Neptune, NJ: T. F. H. Publications, 1979.
- Palmer, Joan. *Reptiles and Amphibians*. Poole, Dorset, UK: Blandford Press, 1983.
- Steinberg, Phil. *Terrarium Pets*. Minneapolis: Lerner Publications, 1979.
- Wexo, John Bonnett. *Alligators & Crocodiles*. Mankato, MN: Creative Education, 1989.

STUFFED FISH

Fish are marvelous creatures, and are great fun to watch and study! Since our earth is covered primarily by water, it's important to know something about the inhabitants of this watery realm. Fish come in a wonderful variety of shapes, colors, and designs. Highly aerodynamic creatures, fish zip through the water much like birds in the air. In this activity, we will focus on some of the amazing qualities of these underwater wonders.

While you are on the topic of fish, you may want to touch on the devastating effects of pollution on marine life. Indeed, with the many waste materials of human technology, we have endangered our oceans, rivers, lakes, and streams. In some places, chemical spills and poor waste disposal have seriously harmed or killed all fish and other marine life. In addition to oil spills and nuclear wastes, over-fishing wreaks havoc on many marine populations.

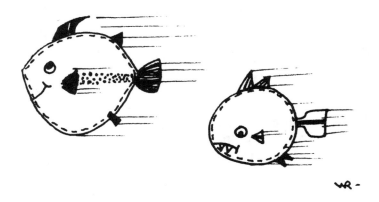

Materials

- 9" x 12" manila paper
- 12" x 18" construction paper of assorted colors
- construction paper scraps
- newspaper
- pencils
- markers
- scissors
- white glue
- staplers and staples

Activity

1. Begin the activity by showing pictures or posters of different kinds of fish. Ask the children whether they have ever gone fishing or if they have an aquarium at home.

2. Next, discuss the fact that fish have a variety of sizes, shapes, colors, and designs. If you have an aquarium in your class-room, ask the kids to look closely at the fish inhabitants.

69

3. Following this discussion, ask each child to choose either a real or an imaginary fish and to make a simple pencil sketch of it on the 9" x 12" manila paper.

4. When the sketch is complete, have each child select two sheets of 12" x 18" construction paper of assorted colors for the body of his/her fish and transfer the designs to the construction paper using pencil.

5. Next, have each child cut out her/his design with scissors and fasten the two fish together by stapling them halfway around the edges. Then have the children cut up some newspaper, open the fish up like a pocket, and begin to stuff it with the paper cuttings. When this is done, they can complete the stapling process. The fattened fish shape is now ready for decoration.

6. Encourage each child to use the assorted construction-paper scraps, glue, and markers to decorate his/her fish with fins, scales, eyes, mouth, and the like.

7. When the fish are complete, hold a fishy discussion and exhibit!

Follow-Up

Make a visit to an aquarium or local pet shop or invite a fish fancier to speak to your class.

Helpful Books

• Harter, Walter. *Deadly Creatures of the Sea.* New York: Parents Magazine Press, 1977.
• Martin, James. *Tentacles.* New York: Crown Publishers, 1993.
• Parks, James. *A Day at the Bottom of the Sea.* New York: Crane Russak, 1977.
• Ricciuti, Edward R. *Fish.* Woodbridge, CT: Blackbirch Pr., Inc., 1993.

LARGE CREATURES

Imagine if everything in the world were the same size! Think how monotonous things would be. Thank goodness that nature exhibits endless variety, and that some creatures are small and others are large. When we think about big animals, which ones spring to mind? Certainly, elephants and whales are two very good choices. And there are lots more! In this activity, we will be concentrating on large animals, and creating imaginative paper sculptures of them.

Materials

- large paper grocery bags
- small paper sandwich bags
- newspaper
- 9" x 12" construction paper of assorted colors
- fluorescent paper
- paper scraps
- yarn
- found objects
- markers
- white glue
- staplers and staples
- scissors

Activity

1. Begin the activity by asking the children to name some large animals that share the planet with us. Make a list of these animals on the board.

2. Explain to the children that we will be creating imaginative replicas of these animals. Show a creature you have made, and briefly describe the following process:

   a. Select the large animal you wish to create.

   b. To form the body, fill a large paper grocery bag with approximately seventeen sheets of crumpled-up newspaper, and staple it shut.

c.   To form the head, fill a small paper sandwich bag with approximately four sheets of crumpled-up newspaper, and staple it shut.

d.   Attach the small bag to the large one using staples and glue.

e.   Cut out feet, tail, ears, eyes, and various bodily decorations using the construction paper, and glue them to the bags. Use the markers to define facial features and enhance designs.

f.   Add yarn and found objects (such as ribbons) to spice up your large creature.

3.   After you have finished your explanation, distribute the materials and let the children begin work. Be sure to encourage them to be imaginative!

4.   When the children have completed their animals, hold a sharing session, and set up a "big" display!

Follow-Up

Ask the children to do some research on large animals of their choice, and to write reports for class. Take a class trip to the zoo to look at some large animals.

Helpful Books

- Carwardine, Mark. *The Illustrated World of Wild Animals.* New York: Simon & Schuster, 1988.
- Rinard, Judith E. *Zoos Without Cages.* Washington, DC: National Geographic Society, 1981.
- Roy, Ron. *Big and Small, Short and Tall.* New York: Clarion Books, 1986.

DRAGONFLIES, FIREFLIES, AND GLOWWORMS

Anyone who has ever been near a pond, lake, or river during warm weather has probably watched dragonflies dart about like miniature helicopters. Many of us have also collected fireflies in a jar on a summer night, or just watched these amazing insects blink their tiny lanterns. Glowworms, phosphorescent insect larvae, may not be as common as these other creatures, but their effect is truly amazing. I remember venturing into a glowworm cave with my family several years ago in New Zealand, and seeing a truly dazzling display of tiny star-like lights. At the slightest noise, the lights would go out—throwing the cave into total darkness! In this activity, we will be creating our own dragonflies, fireflies, or glowworms. The designs we come up with should emphasize imagination and fun! Although we will begin by studying real insects, the creative possibilities suggested by these three creatures are too good to pass up!

Materials

- drinking straws (paper or plastic)
- scraps of construction paper
- 8" x 11" unlined writing paper
- small movable eyes
- sparkles or sequins
- pipe cleaners
- thread
- white glue
- plastic tape
- fine-tipped markers
- scissors

Activity

1. Begin this activity by holding a discussion about dragonflies, fireflies, and glowworms. Let the children tell some stories about these creatures.

2. Briefly show some books about these insects, and make them available for the children to look at.

3. Explain that we will be making our own imaginative versions of these creatures.

4. Before distributing the materials, explain that the straws can be cut down for dragonflies and fireflies. Wings can be cut from folded paper and glued onto the straws. Eyes and legs can also be added. For glowworms, the straws can be connected. Imaginative details can be applied by using the moveable plastic eyes, pipe cleaners, sparkles, and markers.

5. Distribute the materials and invite each child to make her/his own insect.

6. When the creations are finished, discuss and display them. By adding thread, the insects can be suspended from shelves, window handles, and the like.

Follow-Up

Ask the children to do reports on the creatures they have made. If you own a "dragonfly lens" (a special magnifying glass), bring it to class and let the children look through it! Invite a speaker in to discuss insects.

Helpful Books

- Armour, Richard. *Insects All Around Us.* New York: McGraw-Hill, 1981.
- Overbeck, Cynthia. *Dragonflies.* Minneapolis: Lerner Publications, 1982.
- Parker, Steve. *Insects.* New York: Dorling Kindersley, 1992.
- Russo, Monica. *The Insect Almanac.* New York: Sterling Publishing, 1991.

CREATURES OF THE AIR

Birds are truly marvelous creatures, with the magical ability to soar high above the Earth. They exhibit tremendous variation in size, color, and design. Anyone who has a simple bird-feeder is able to watch some of these creatures at closer range. Depending upon one's geographic location, an amazing array of other birds, from seagulls to eagles, and from crows to owls can also be seen! In this activity, we will study real birds, then create and decorate some bird designs of our own. Before starting the activity, head for the library, and check out some materials on our feathered friends. Bring this information to class, to help enhance your lesson.

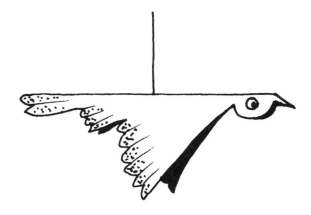

Materials

- 9" x 12" newsprint paper
- 12" x 18" construction paper of assorted colors
- paper scraps
- pencils
- crayons
- markers
- yarn
- white glue
- scissors
- hole punches

Activity

1. Start the activity by holding a discussion on birds and showing some pictures and books about these fascinating creatures. Ask the students how many of them have birds as pets.

2. Explain that we will be investigating birds and designing our own creative editions of these aerodynamic wonders.

3. Hold a brief demonstration on cutting a symmetrical bird shape in the following manner:

   a. Fold a 12" x 18" sheet of construction paper in half, either the long or short way.

b. Lightly sketch half the bird shape using pencil.

c. Holding the fold, cut carefully along the pencil lines, and open the resulting shape to form the complete bird.

d. Decorate the bird shape using paper scraps and markers.

e. Punch two holes in your shape, and string it with yarn for hanging in the following way:

4. After completing the demonstration, distribute the 9" x 12" newsprint paper, and let the children begin to formulate some sketches using pencil. Encourage originality. Each bird shape should be unique, reflecting the individual choices of each child.

5. When children have settled on their favorite design, distribute the rest of the materials, and let them create their own creatures of the air.

6. At the conclusion of the activity, hold a bird discussion and display.

Follow-Up

Have the children prepare reports on birds of their choice by researching them in the classroom or school library. Invite a bird-watcher to speak to the class, and/or take a trip to a local zoo or bird sanctuary.

Helpful Books

- Boulton, Carolyn. *Birds.* New York: Franklin Watts, 1984.
- Saunders, David. *Sea Birds.* New York: Grosset & Dunlap, 1973.
- Sill, Cathryn. *About Birds.* Atlanta: Peachtree Publishers, 1991.
- Singer, Marilyn. *Exotic Birds.* New York: Doubleday, 1990.

An Undersea Adventure

Many large cities have public aquariums, where visitors can gaze into the amazing world beneath the surface of the water. The diverse forms of sealife inhabiting this realm are still being discovered and explored. Although many of us may never have had an underwater experience or been to a major aquarium, a trip to the local pet shop, to gaze into the many aquariums, is a great alternative. There, in miniature form, one can gain a partial picture of the great underwater world. If your classroom has its own aquarium, students can venture under water without leaving the room. You may wish to gather pictures and books from the library to further embellish the experience.

Materials

- 9" x 12" newsprint paper
- 12" x 18" white drawing paper
- pencils
- crayons
- watercolors
- brushes
- water
- water cups
- paper towels
- newspaper

Activity

1. Start the activity by introducing the idea of an undersea adventure. Ask the children if they have ever been snorkeling or scuba diving, or visited a large aquarium. How many children have aquariums at home? Hold a discussion on these topics.

2. Next, make a list on the chalkboard of possible fish and other marine life we might encounter under water. Show pictures or books to fortify the list.

77

3. Ask the children to pretend they are on a special undersea expedition. Perhaps they are in a submarine or living in an underwater village of the future like the one in Epcot Center (Disney World, Florida). Encourage each child to make a pencil drawing on the 9" x 12" newsprint paper of his/her own undersea adventure. Remind students that they can consult the list of items on the chalkboard for ideas.

4. When the sketches are complete, distribute the 12" x 18" white drawing paper and crayons, and have the children make their final drawings. Tell the kids to use the crayons primarily for outlining basic shapes, not for coloring in, and to leave lots of white space.

5. After the crayon drawings are complete, dispense the rest of the materials, and let the children paint over their crayon drawings with watercolors. To cover a large area with paint, it's a good idea to create a "wash," by first painting the area with water, and then brushing some color into the moist spot.

6. The resulting "crayon resist works" let the crayon lines shine through the watercolor in a very special way!

7. When the paintings are dry, hold a sharing session and exhibit.

Follow-Up

Take a class trip to a large aquarium or visit a local pet store. Invite a guest speaker who is knowledgeable about fish or scuba diving to address the class.

Helpful Books

- Martin, James. *Tentacles.* New York: Crown Publishers, 1993.
- Parks, James. *A Day at the Bottom of the Sea.* New York: Crane Russak, 1977.
- Ricciuti, Edward R. *Fish.* Woodbridge, CT: Blackbirch, Pr., 1993.
- Ryder, Willet. *The Art Experience.* Glenview, IL: GoodYearBooks, 1991.

America is dotted with national parks, from the Atlantic to the Pacific, and from the Canadian Border to the Gulf of Mexico. Each park is unique and preserves the special characteristics of the specific geographic area. Whether the parklands are composed of rugged ocean coastline or majestic canyons, national parks are a national treasure!

Usually, one need not journey far from home to find a park. Some local parks may be just around the corner or down the street. Others, such as New York's amazing Central Park, are right in the midst of major cities.

During July, we will be celebrating our parks and the many recreational opportunities they offer! We will be learning about some local and national parks. We will be planting a tree and designing our ideal tent for camping. We will also be doing activities related to hiking, biking, and swimming. In short, we will be sampling a range of summer projects that center around our parklands.

The summer sun is just beginning to rise, and the day is ripe with possibilities. Let's grab our knapsacks and be off!

A JOURNEY TO A LOCAL PARK

I'll bet your town or city has a local park that is not very far from where you live. It may have grass and trees, or sand and cactus plants. Perhaps it has winding paths, flower gardens, and benches, or maybe a small pond or gazebo. Most of us are probably aware of such a park. We may have had a picnic at this park, listened to a concert there on a warm summer night, or just bicycled down its paths.

In this activity, we will be visiting a local park and making some drawings of it. Before introducing the topic to your students, take a trip to the park and scout out the area. How will you get the children there? Is it within walking distance or will a school bus be required? When is the best time to go? Should the children bring lunch? Needless to say, don't forget to clear the date with your principal, arrange for chaperones, and prepare and obtain parental permission slips. It is also very important to discuss precautions against Lyme Disease in certain areas of the country.

Since the trip will involve making drawings, be sure to bring enough art materials and plastic garbage bags for cleaning up trash. Before starting on the trip, explain to the children that they will be making some drawings of some of the things they notice at the park.

Materials

- 9" x 12" newsprint and white drawing paper
- 12" x 12" corrugated cardboard sheets
- pencils
- pens
- markers
- wet paper towels
- dry paper towels
- notebooks
- bag lunches
- picnic blankets
- plastic garbage bags

Activity

1. When trip day arrives and the class is at the park, split up into small chaperoned groups and take a walk around. Ask the children to carefully observe things that interest them.

2. Next, have the members of each group settle on benches or picnic blankets. Distribute the cardboard sheets (used to rest paper on), paper, pencils, and markers, so that students can begin making drawings of intriguing objects they see. These might include rocks, trees, flowers, and the like. Encourage the children to look closely at these things and create their own original drawings. The style they select is up to them.

3. When the drawings are complete, dispense the notebooks and pens, and ask the children to write a short composition about the trip.

4. Collect the drawings and compositions, and enjoy the rest of the day with picnics and games.

5. Hold a sharing session and exhibit the works when you return to school.

Follow-Up

Discuss what the children enjoyed about the trip, and ask them for suggestions or ideas on how the park could be improved.

Helpful Books

- Aska, Warabe. *Who Goes to the Park?* Montreal, Quebec: Tundra Books, 1984.
- Coats, Laura Jane. *Marcella and the Moon.* New York: Macmillan Publishing Company, 1986.
- Ernst, Lisa Campbell. *Squirrel Park.* New York: Bradbury Press, 1993.

81

PLANTING A TREE

Trees are like special gifts—gifts that help people enjoy more healthful and comfortable lives. They also enhance the environment, making it a place of great beauty and excitement. In the cooler regions of North America, trees become colorful messengers of autumn. In warmer climates, palm trees not only provide needed shade, but also supply fruit and material for shelter. Every tree, in fact, has a special purpose and mission.

The goal of this activity is to learn more about trees. We will be planting a tree to help beautify the school grounds, and we will be creating torn paper tree designs. Before introducing the idea of planting a tree to your class, be sure to discuss it with the school principal and obtain his/her approval.

Materials

- 9" x 12" colored construction paper
- construction paper scraps
- white glue

Activity

1. No matter where we live, chances are that when we look out a window we see at least one tree. Talk about trees with the children, and encourage them to join in the discussion.

2. Ask some questions about trees. Why are trees important to people? How many fruits come from trees? What holidays are associated with trees? How are trees beneficial?

3. Explain that in this activity, we will be learning more about trees, selecting and planting a "class tree," and making tree designs.

82

4. Following is the suggested procedure for tree planting:

   a. Show the class some pictures of different types of trees, and ask them to select their favorite. Take a class vote to determine the final tree choice.

   b. Visit a local nursery and find out the price of the selected tree. It is possible that the nursery may be willing to donate a tree to your class, so don't forget to ask!

   c. After obtaining the price, divide the total cost across your class. Either collect this amount from each child, or raise money in a fund-raising effort such as a bake sale.

   d. Next, arrange a delivery date for the tree, and obtain information about planting and watering it. Share this information with the children prior to actually planting the tree.

   e. On "Planting Day," be sure to bring a camera, shovel, water, and the like. Bring the children to the planting site (preselected by the school administration), and plant and water the new tree. Keep in mind that the tree could be planted in honor or in memory of someone important to the school.

5. When you return to class, do a torn paper design using the colored construction paper and white glue. Encourage each child to create a tree, and use hands, not scissors, to tear out his/her design.

6. When the designs are complete, discuss the tree planting and exhibit the artwork.

Follow-Up

Ask the children to investigate trees and write compositions about them. The theme might be "Trees Are Good Friends!" Invite a tree expert or specialist from a local nursery or greenhouse, to your class to speak about trees.

Helpful Books

- Arnold, Caroline. *The Biggest Living Thing*. Minneapolis: Carolrhoda Books, 1983.
- Arnosky, Jim. *Crinkleroot's Guide to Knowing the Trees*. New York: Bradbury Press, 1992.
- Markle, Sandra. *Outside and Inside Trees*. New York: Bradbury Press, 1993.
- Silverstein, Shel. *The Giving Tree*. New York: HarperCollins Childrens Books, 1964.

83

LEARNING ABOUT A NATIONAL PARK

Our national parks are, without a doubt, national treasures. They include parks both on land and under water, and extend across our country in every direction, preserving a sample of natural America. People from around the country and around the world can hike down wooded trails, marvel at great mountains and spectacular vistas, and catch a glimpse of desert or ocean life. The National Park Service is happy to supply a listing of parks around the country, with directions on how to reach them.

It is difficult to measure the full effect of national parks on the population. One could certainly say, however, that national parks satisfy a real longing for the simple life outside the walls and windows of our modern technical world.

In this activity, we will be looking at some wonderful parks and creating individual travel posters to honor them. Before introducing the activity, collect some materials on national parks. These might include posters, books, brochures, and maps.

Yosemite

Materials

- 9" x 12" newsprint paper
- 12" x 18" colored posterboard
- pencils
- markers
- tempera paint
- brushes
- paint cups
- water
- newspapers
- paper towels

Activity

1. Start out by showing children the materials you collected on national parks and asking some general questions. Who has been to a national park? Where was it located? What did you see?

2. Briefly discuss these parks, and invite the children to look through the information you have available.

3. Briefly review the highlights of creating a travel poster, and list them on the chalkboard:

   a. Keep the picture or illustration simple.

   b. Keep the message simple.

   c. Make the lettering clear. (Discuss guidelines for lettering.)

4. Next, ask each child to select a park and design a travel poster about it. Distribute the newsprint paper and pencils, and let the children start making sketches.

5. When the sketches are finished, ask the children to transfer their designs to the 12" x 18" posterboard using pencils, markers, and paint.

6. After the artworks have been completed, hold a discussion and poster display.

Follow-Up

If you happen to live near a national park, you may wish to arrange to display the class artwork at park headquarters. Invite a park ranger from this park to speak to your class. Take a class trip to the national park in your area.

Helpful Books

- Brownstone, David M., and Franck, Irene M. *Natural Wonders of America.* New York: Atheneum, 1989.
- National Geographic Society. *Adventures in Your National Parks.* Washington, DC: National Geographic Society, 1988.
- National Geographic Society. *Nature's Wonderlands—National Parks of the World.* Washington, DC: National Geographic Society, 1989.
- Patent, Dorothy Hinshaw. *Places of Refuge—Our National Wildlife Refuge System.* New York: Clarion Books, 1992.

HIKING AND BIKING

When the weather is nice, and it's warm and sunny, most of us think about getting outside! Two very popular forms of summer recreation are hiking and biking. Both of these exciting activities can be as easy or strenuous as you wish. Hiking can consist of a pleasant walk or be a major backpacking adventure into the wilderness. Biking can be a simple ride to town for an ice cream soda or a long-distance trip that follows a complicated route.

In this activity, we will be creating simple maps for an ideal hike or bike ride. These maps can be completely fictitious or can be based on actual places you have seen or those you would like to visit.

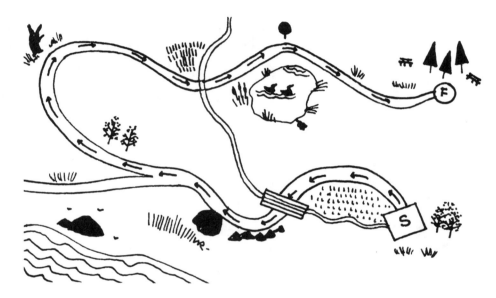

Materials

- 8" x 11" composition paper
- 9" x 12" newsprint paper
- 9" x 12" white drawing paper
- pencils
- rulers
- markers
- crayons

Activity

1. Ask the class a few questions to launch this activity. Have any of you ever been on a hike? How many of you own bicycles? Hold a brief discussion on these topics.

2. Next, ask the children to imagine a hike or bike ride that they have taken or would like to take. Distribute the composition paper, and invite the children to make a list of some of the things they have noticed or hope to see on their trip. These might include mountains, canyons, streets, roads, trails, brooks, forests, a seashore, and the like.

3. Distribute the newsprint paper and pencils, and ask each child to begin to create a sketch of his/her own hiking or biking map using the list as a guide. Suggest that each child label a "starting point," design her/his own route, and then identify a "finishing point." The route should include simple drawings of the things the children listed. Trails and roads can be indicated with different colored lines and arrows.

4. After the sketches are complete, mention to the children that they may wish to add a map legend and/or a directional indicator (compass rose). Briefly discuss these items.

5. Next, distribute the white drawing paper and other materials, and ask the children to transfer and color their designs.

6. When all the maps have been completed, hold a sharing session and exhibition.

Follow-Up

Organize a class hike or bike ride. Invite an avid hiker or biker to speak to your class and show some slides of her/his adventures.

Helpful Books

- Coombs, Charles. *All-Terrain Bicycling.* New York: Henry Holt, 1987.
- Foster, Lynne. *Take a Hike!* San Francisco: Sierra Club Books, 1991.
- McManus, Patrick F. Kid *Camping from Aaaaiii to ZIP.* New York: Lothrop, Lee & Shepard, 1979.
- Mohn, Peter B. *Hiking.* Mankato, MN: Crestwood House, 1975.
- Murphy, Jim. *Two Hundred Years of Bicycles.* New York: J. B. Lippincott, 1983.
- Stine, Megan. *Wheels! The Kids' Bike Book.* Boston: Sports Illustrated for Kids Books, 1990.

SWIMMING: TAKING THE PLUNGE!

Swimming can be a real "splash" and is probably one of the most refreshing forms of summer recreation. Although not everyone is a swimmer, most of us enjoy the feeling of at least dipping our toes in cool water on a very hot day!

Birds often enjoy a good swim. If you happen to live near the seashore, as I do, you may have noticed a variety of birds paddling about. These include sea gulls, terns, cormorants, ducks, geese, and swans. Some of these birds, such as cormorants, even like to dive under the water.

In this activity, we will be celebrating water and swimming, by designing our own small seabirds. Before starting to work with your class, be sure to collect a good supply of styrofoam. Rather than purchase this material, you can usually get ample amounts by collecting packing materials—especially styrofoam panels and boxes—used for cushioning objects during shipping.

Materials

- styrofoam packaging material (1/2" to 3/4" thick)
- toothpicks
- colored tapes
- pencils
- markers
- scissors
- plastic picnic knives

Activity

1. Discuss the topic of swimming, letting the children relate some of their experiences.

2. Ask them some questions about birds that swim. What kind of birds swim? How do they navigate?

3. List some swimming birds on the chalkboard, and explain that we will be making our own miniature swimming birds.

4. Ask each child to select a bird from the list or make up one of his/her own. Review the following steps for making a styrofoam bird:

a. Using a piece of styrofoam, lightly draw the general shape of your bird, as seen from above, with pencil.

b. On another piece of styrofoam, lightly draw the shape of the bird's head, as seen from the side.

c. Carefully cut (in a saw-like motion) the two shapes from the styrofoam, using a plastic picnic knife.

d. Decorate these two shapes by cutting small pieces of colored tape with your scissors and applying them to the styrofoam pieces.

e. Add eyes and other details using markers.

f. Attach the two pieces together using sections of broken toothpicks.

g. When the head has been connected to the body, your bird is ready to take the plunge!

5. Distribute the materials to the children and let them go to work.

6. When the birds are finished, put a few inches of water in the bottom of a large plastic pan, and let the kids float their creations.

Follow-Up

Invite a swimming coach or lifeguard to speak to the children about swimming and water safety.

Helpful Books

- Gorton, Eddie. *Swimming.* London: Batsford Academic and Educational Ltd., 1982.
- Noble, Jim. *Swimming.* New York: The Bookwright Press, 1991.
- Saunders, David. *Sea Birds.* New York: Grosset & Dunlap, 1973.
- Wexo, John Bonnett. *Ducks, Geese & Swans.* Mankato, MN: Creative Education, 1989.

DESIGNING A TENT

Anyone who has ever slept in a tent knows the special feeling of camping. That such a fragile covering of cloth can protect one against the elements is indeed a wonderful concept. Over the years, our family has pitched our small umbrella tent on mountain sides, as well as on the sandy desert floor and grassy prairie. We have also observed the tent dwellers, such as the Bedouins in the Mideast.

Tents are both convenient and portable, enabling users to be at a different "address" every night if they wish, yet still live in the same "house." Sadly, some people in our own country live in tent cities—due to natural disasters or poverty. Tents come in a wide variety of shapes, sizes, and color schemes. We will be focusing on these design aspects in this activity. Before introducing the activity, acquaint yourself with tents by taking a trip to a nearby sporting goods or camping store. You might also check out books from your local library. If you have done some camping, gather some pictures and slides of the experience. Remember to bring any materials you have collected on tents with you to class.

Materials

- 9" x 12" newsprint paper
- 9" x 12" white drawing paper
- pencils
- rulers
- markers
- crayons

Activity

1. Ask the children if they have ever been camping or slept in a tent. Spend some time discussing these experiences. What type of organization conducts most of its business in a tent? Briefly discuss the circus and circus tents.

2. Explain that in this activity, each child will be designing her/his own imaginative tent. These tents may be based on actual tent designs or can be completely new and original.

90

3. Show some of the information you have collected on tents, and hold a short discussion.

4. Next, distribute the newsprint paper and ask the children to make some sketches of their ideal tents. Remind the children that the tents can be decorated with colorful patterns and designs.

5. Invite each child to select his/her favorite sketch and transfer it to the white drawing paper. The designs can be colored in using crayons and markers.

6. When the tent designs are finished, hold a discussion and arrange for a tent exhibit.

Follow-Up

Invite a guest speaker from a local hiking group or camping association to speak to the class about tenting. If you have a small tent, bring it to class and demonstrate how to set it up!

Helpful Books

- Neimark, Paul. *Camping and Ecology.* Chicago: Childrens Press, 1981.
- Stokes, Jack. *Let's Make a Tent.* New York: David McKay Company, 1979.

Close your eyes for a few moments, and imagine the world with no water. Picture a dry and parched landscape filled with sand and rocks, where life, as we know it, would be impossible. Such a place would be drier than our most arid desert—a mean, unfriendly region!

Luckily for all of us, water is present on our planet, enabling plants, animals, and human beings to thrive. We all must realize, however, how valuable water is and be watchful that it remains pure and unpolluted. Guarding our water and maintaining its quality are very important missions. Just think, some places in the world contain little or no water; in other places, the water is unfit to drink.

During the month of August, we will be considering different aspects of water. We will be sampling this remarkable resource and trying to make others more aware of its value.

We will be traveling to a water company, as well as creating some designs. We will also be designing a fountain and making some drawings while we listen to water-inspired music. It makes me thirsty just thinking of all these things! So, let's grab a glass and consider the wonders of water.

WATER: IT'S EASY TO SWALLOW!

Have you ever walked a long distance on a very hot day and gotten the urge for a giant glass of cold water? Perhaps you have looked across a desert or down a long highway on such a day and thought, for a moment, that you saw a pool of water—only to discover it was just a mirage. Without water, we'd all be up the creek! Indeed, this liquid resource is vital to life on our planet.

In this activity, we will be sampling some water and drawing our feelings as they relate to thirst. Before starting the activity, go to your local supermarket and purchase some bottled water and paper or plastic cups.

Materials

- bottled water
- paper or plastic cups
- 9" x 12" manila paper
- crayons

Activity

1. Launch a class discussion about water and why it is important. Not only is much of our planet covered by water, but human beings are largely composed of this vital element. Briefly discuss the water cycle and the value of water.

2. Next, ask the children how it feels to be thirsty. Encourage them to discuss some of their experiences.

3. Explain that in a few minutes, we will be sampling some water. During this sampling session, ask the kids to be thinking carefully about the qualities of water and thirst.

4. Distribute the cups and water, and let the children enjoy a drink. Then, dispense the drawing paper and crayons, and invite each

child to draw her/his feelings about thirst. The drawings can be rendered in any style the children wish.

5. When the artworks are complete, hold a brief sharing session and exhibit.

Follow-Up

Discuss the fact that there are different types of water. These include fresh water, salt water, spring water, and mineral water. Bring a bottle of mineral water to class, and let the children sample this bubbling delight. Invite the children to do some research on water and write compositions about this wonderful resource.

Helpful Books

- Barkan, Joanne. *Water, Water Everywhere.* New York: Silver Press, 1990.
- Branley, Franklyn M. *Water for the World.* New York: T. Y. Crowell, 1982.
- McClymont, Diane. *Water.* Ada, OK: Garrett Educational Corporation, 1991.

SAVE OUR H₂O

Since we could not exist on earth without H_2O, the message of this activity is to establish ways to conserve and save our water supply. How many of us let the water run into the sink while we brush our teeth, or use gallons of water sprinkling our lawns to achieve just the right shade of green? On a broader scale, some industries follow unsafe dumping practices, polluting our groundwater and rivers; others spray crops and shrubbery with chemicals that eventually reach our water supply.

What can we do about these things? How can we make people more aware of such harmful practices? As teachers, we are all dedicated to the value of a sound education in changing the behavior of people for the better. Helping children become more aware of ways to save our water supply, and showing them how to influence others, is a step in the right direction.

In this activity, you will be calling on children to devise posters that focus on ways to save water. The posters should be simple and to the point. They should contain a minimum of words and a maximum of design impact!

Materials

- 9" x 12" manila paper
- 12" x 18" colored posterboard and colored construction paper
- white glue
- pencils
- markers
- rulers
- scissors

From *Celebrating Diversity with Art: Thematic Projects for Every Month of the Year*, published by GoodYearBooks. Copyright © 1995 by Willet Ryder.

Activity

1. Hold a discussion on the importance of keeping our water safe. Why is safe drinking water important? What are some ways you can think of to conserve water and keep it pure? Make a list of the children's suggestions on the chalkboard.

2. Invite each child to look over the list and select one point that interests her/him.

3. After the children have made their selections, distribute the 9" x 12" manila paper and pencils, and ask them to make some sketches to illustrate their idea. Remind them to keep the sketches simple, and not to make the message too long!

4. When the sketches are complete, distribute the rest of the materials, and let the students put their final designs on the posterboard using cut paper and markers. Remind students to use pencil guidelines for all lettering, and carefully review spelling as needed.

5. When the posters are complete, be sure to hold a sharing session and exhibit.

Follow-Up

Invite a speaker from a government conservation agency (local, state, or national) to address the class on the issue of water pollution and conservation. Arrange to exhibit the children's artwork in the local library or bank to help spread the word.

Helpful Books

- Corliss, Mark. *Focus on Water.* Hove, East Sussex, England: Wayland Publishers Ltd., 1985.
- Lucas, Eileen. *Water: A Resource in Crisis.* Chicago: Childrens Press, 1991.
- Sauvain, Philip. *Water—The Way It Works.* New York: New Discovery Books, 1992.

A Trip to a Water Company

A water company is an interesting organization whose job it is to get the purest water to your home. Besides maintaining the quality of water, such companies are in charge of water storage facilities, such as reservoirs and water storage tanks, and the pumping stations and pipes that get the water to our houses and apartments. In large urban and suburban areas, where there are lots of people, water companies are quite common. However, if you live in the country, chances are that you have your own well and pumping equipment. In such cases, you're your own water company!

If your school is located in a fairly populated area, your water is probably supplied by a company. If you're not familiar with the water company that services your school, check the yellow pages under "water companies—utility." Arrange a short field trip to the company, so that the children can learn more about water and how a water company functions.

Materials

- notebooks
- sketchbooks
- pencils
- pens

Activity

1. Check with the local water company, and arrange a field-trip day. Be sure to clear the date with your principal, obtain parental permission for each child to attend, and arrange for transportation and chaperones.

2. Ask the company to send you some information prior to the trip, which you can discuss with your class.

3. When trip day arrives, enjoy the outing!

4. When the class returns to school, ask the children to write compositions about what impressed them about the trip. In addition, invite them to make drawings about one aspect of this journey, to help illustrate what they've written.

5. Hold a discussion and display these writings and artworks.

Follow-Up

Invite a well driller, or a water company or bottled water representative to class to discuss their job.

Helpful Books

- Cobb, Vicki. *The Trip of a Drip.* Boston: Little, Brown, 1986.
- Johnston, Tom. *Water, Water!* Milwaukee: Gareth Stevens, 1988.
- Lefkowitz, R. J. *Water for Today and Tomorrow.* New York: Parents' Magazine Press, 1973.

ABSTRACT BUBBLE DESIGNS

Anyone who has ever walked along the seashore or taken a dunk in the ocean or a fast-moving brook has seen plenty of foam and bubbles. Jacuzzis and hot tubs are also filled with these natural wonders. If you have ever added too much detergent when washing dishes or clothes, you've probably created lots of bubbles.

Remember the bottles of liquid soap we all used to blow bubbles with as children, and the mysterious iridescent quality of those floating creations? In this activity, we will be focusing on bubbles and making abstract designs based upon them. Before starting, be sure to pick up a good supply of liquid soap and bubble wands for your class.

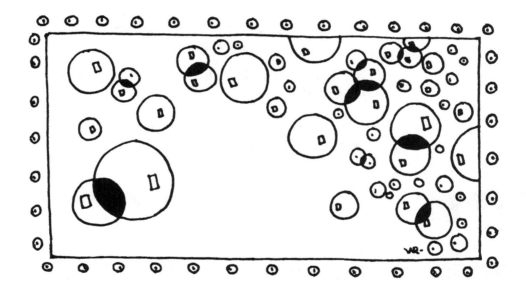

Materials

- bottles of liquid soap
- bubble wands
- 9" x 12" white drawing paper
- pencils
- crayons
- markers

Activity

1. Ask the children where they have noticed "bubbles" in nature. Discuss the many places we might see these gorgeous globes—for example, the seashore, bathtub or dishpan.

2. Explain that in this activity, we will be concentrating on bubbles! Tell the children that in a short time, we will all go outside and create some bubbles. Remind them to carefully observe the bubbles as they float about!

3. Next, take a walk outside to the playing field, and distribute the liquid soap and wands. Let the children enjoy blowing bubbles for a short while.

4. Collect the materials and return to the classroom. Then, hold a brief discussion about what the children observed.

5. Next, invite the students to make bubble designs based on their experiences. Explain that the bubbles they draw can be in various sizes and can overlap one another. The designs can also be infinite, stretching off the drawing paper in all directions, like this:

6. Distribute the drawing paper, pencils, crayons, and markers and let the kids get to work!

7. When the designs are complete, hold a bubble exhibit. You might wish to serve "sparkling water" at the exhibit opening!

Follow-Up

Invite the children to do research on bubbles and write compositions about them!

Helpful Books

- Lorimer, Janet. *The Biggest Bubble in the World.* New York: Franklin Watts, 1982.
- Seed, Deborah. *Water Science.* Reading, MA: Addison-Wesley, 1992.
- Walpole, Brenda. *Water.* New York: Warwick Press, 1987.
- Zubrowski, Bernie. *A Children's Museum Activity Book: Bubbles.* Boston: Little, Brown, 1979.

DESIGNING A PUBLIC FOUNTAIN

In many places in the world, spectacular public fountains form the centerpiece of parks and city squares. The wonderful fountains of Rome or London serve as excellent examples. Many of the large cities in our own country have public fountains, as well, where people gather to cool off, eat a sandwich, talk to a friend, or just enjoy a nice day. This is also true in some small towns, where the fountain square may serve as the center of activity.

There is something almost magical about bubbling, spouting, and cascading water. Perhaps it has to do with the fine spray of a fountain carried on a light breeze or the prismatic effects of sunlight on gushing water. Everyone, from small children to older adults, seems to take delight in fountains.

In this activity, we will be designing public fountains for a city or town setting. The fountains can have realistic or abstract plants, animals, and people, steps of cascading water, or giant plumes of spray. They can be small in size or quite monumental. You may wish to visit your local library before introducing this activity to the children, to obtain some books and pictures about public fountains. If you have any pictures or slides of your own, bring them with you to class when you're ready to begin.

Materials

- 9" x 12" manila paper and white drawing paper
- pencils
- markers
- rulers
- watercolors
- brushes
- water cups
- water
- newspaper
- paper towels

Activity

1. Introduce the topic of public fountains to the class, and hold a discussion about them. How many of you have ever seen a public fountain? What did it look like?

2. Show some books, pictures, and slides of public fountains and briefly discuss them.

3. Ask each child to pretend that he/she is an architect and has been hired to design a public fountain. Distribute the 9" x 12" manila paper and pencils, and have everybody sketch their ideas for such a project.

4. Next, have each child select her/his favorite idea. Dispense the rest of the materials, and ask the children to transfer their designs to the white drawing paper. They can color and paint the drawings using the markers and watercolors.

5. When the designs are complete, hold a sharing session and exhibit.

Follow-Up

Invite an architect or landscape designer to your class to explain how she/he works. Take a class trip to a nearby public fountain.

Helpful Books

- Ledbetter, Gordon T. *Water Gardens.* New York: W. W. Norton, 1979.
- Robinson, Peter. *Pool and Waterside Gardening.* Twickenham, Middlesex, England: Collingridge Books, 1987.

102

DRAWING TO WATER MUSIC

Living on the south shore of Long Island, close to the Great South Bay and the Atlantic Ocean, I try to visit both of these bodies of water as much as possible. There is something exhilarating about water, no matter how often I see it, swim in it, or walk along its shores! Water has the power to soothe and inspire, to show ferocious strength or quiet repose!

In this activity, we will be picturing water as we listen to musical selections that celebrate this great resource. There are many fine pieces of music that have water as their theme. Three of my favorites are "The Water Music Suite" by G. F. Handel, "The Sea" by Vaughan Williams, and "Le Mer" by C. Debussy. Of course, you probably have your own favorites. You might also consider some of the intriguing environmental tapes of water sounds. Before introducing this activity in class, locate a selection of music or musical sounds you would enjoy sharing with your students.

Materials

- audio selections of music or sounds about water
- tape recorder, CD player, etc.
- 12" x 18" manila paper
- crayons
- markers
- colored chalks
- paper towels

103

Activity

1. Explain to your class that we will soon be listening to some music or sounds about water. Ask the children to listen carefully to these audio selections and to let the sounds suggest visual images.

2. Be sure to point out that the visual ideas may come in any number of different styles. The image, for example, might appear as a picture of a pond or ocean, or it might be a series of squiggly lines and dots of different sizes and colors.

3. Next, distribute the paper, crayons, markers, and/or chalks, and let the music play! Encourage children to draw as they listen, recording whatever images come to mind.

4. When the audio session is finished, hold a sharing period and exhibit the "waterworks."

Follow-Up

Ask the children to listen to these selections again and write a poem based upon them. Exhibit the poems alongside the drawings. The children may become interested in one of the composers. If so, have them do some research and write a short composition on his/her life.

Helpful Books

- Ardley, Neil. *Sound and Music.* New York: Franklin Watts, 1984.
- Richardson, Wendy and Jack. *Water: Through the Eyes of Artists.* Chicago: Childrens Press, 1991.
- Sargent, Sarah. *Watermusic.* New York: Clarion Books, 1986.

¡Hola amigos y amigas! ¡Bienvenidos! Welcome to National Hispanic Heritage Month. America has a long history of association with Spain and with the various Hispanic cultures related to her. The oldest U.S. city, St. Augustine, Florida, was founded by Spanish explorers, as were many settlements along the "Mission Trail" in California. Spanish names identify many of our states and cities, mountains and rivers. Indeed, the Spanish language flourishes in many areas of our land. The fantastic influences of Hispanic culture in terms of language, foods, artwork, and music abound.

During this month, we will be working on a number of activities related to Hispanic culture. We will be designing and creating piñatas and musical instruments. We will be imagining the world's largest tortilla and making artworks about it! We will be holding a small fiesta, playing a language game, and making some molas. So grab your sombrero, and let's be off on an adventure to sample some of the many delights of National Hispanic Heritage Month.

PIÑATAS

Piñatas are great party treats signaling fun and festivities. Since they come in a wide variety of shapes and colors, you can probably select your favorite in any well-stocked party shop. In Mexico, these colorful papier-maché creations are usually filled with candy and suspended from the ceiling; children line up, get blindfolded, and take a crack at breaking the piñata with a long pole.

Piñatas don't have to be filled with candy and broken open at a party, however. The fact is that they make excellent decorations if they are simply displayed in a room. The bright tissue paper and whimsical designs of these wonderful creations are lots of fun to look at!

In this activity, we will be designing and creating piñatas. Keep in mind that such an activity takes time; it will require a number of sessions in order to do it right. To reduce the number of piñatas in progress, you may wish to divide the class into groups of four and let each group create one piñata, rather than have each student do his/her own.

Materials

- one package of paper lunch bags (approximately 100 bags)
- newspapers
- paper bowls
- one bag of flour (5 lbs.)
- water
- plastic bucket
- masking tape
- colored tissue paper
- colored construction paper
- yarn
- found objects
- scissors
- white glue
- colored markers
- steel wire (small piece)
- fishing line or string

Activity

1. Begin the activity by discussing piñatas and showing a few examples.

2. Explain that we will be making these 3-D objects over the course of several class sessions. The first step is for each student or group to decide upon a particular subject for their piñata. Subjects might include birds, fish, animals, and the like.

3. After the themes have been selected, but before distributing the materials, describe the following procedure for creating a piñata:

   a. Cover your workspace with newspaper.

   b. Next, stuff a paper lunch bag with 3 sheets of crumpled up newspaper.

   c. To mix the paste, fill a large bucket about half full of water and mix in some flour, forming a smooth, soupy mixture. (The teacher should serve as the chief mixer!)

   d. Rip several sheets of newspaper into tiny strips for dipping into the paste.

   e. To cover the bag, gently coat it with papier-maché paste. Then dip each newspaper strip into the paste and smooth it onto the surface of the bag. Try to cover all sides of the bag (to about the halfway point), applying the wet strips in different directions.

   f. Put the bag aside to dry, and begin working on the head, if your pinata requires a separate one. Heads can be made by rolling or crumpling up some newspaper, taping it to secure the shape, and covering it with papier-maché.

   g. When the body and head are dry, they can be attached together first with tape, then papier-machéd into place. Add candy at this point, if you wish, through the bag opening. The bag can then be folded, taped, and papier-machéd closed.

   h. To install a hook for suspending the piñata, first find the balance point of your creation. Then, bend a small piece of steel wire into the following shape (Ω), tape it to the piñata, and papier-maché it into place. Later, when you've finished decorating your piñata, you can attach strong string or fishing line to the piñata and hang it up.

i. When the piñata is completely dry, it can be decorated with colored tissue paper, colored construction paper, markers, and found objects.

4. After explaining this procedure completely, begin to distribute the materials and let the work begin.

5. When the piñatas are finished, hold a sharing session. Display the piñatas or save them for a class fiesta.

Follow-Up

Ask the children to write a poem about their piñatas. Encourage them to search for some books about these fun-filled creations. Invite a class parent or grandparent, who may be familiar with piñatas, to tell a story about them to the class.

Helpful Books

- Brock, Virginia. *Piñatas.* Nashville, NY: Abingdon Press, 1966.
- Pals, Ellen M. *Create A Celebration.* Littleton, CO: Aladdin Publishing Company, 1990.
- Purdy, Susan. *Festivals for You to Celebrate.* Philadelphia: J. B. Lippincott, 1969.

CREATING MUSICAL INSTRUMENTS

We have all heard maracas, tambourines, and castanets used in making Latin music. Yet some of us may not be familiar with Chilean rain sticks. These interesting objects can be found in some nature stores, where a wide variety of ecological and aesthetic items from around the world are usually on sale.

I first became aware of rain sticks when photographer Stephen Golding, my brother-in-law, sent me one as a gift. The package had been delivered while we were out. When I picked up the package and tilted it, it sounded as if the contents were broken in a thousand pieces. After removing the wrapping, I found a light brown cylinder, about 3 feet in length, which looked like part of an old cactus plant. It was completely sealed at both ends, and when turned upside down or shaken, it emitted a sound like falling rain. What a great creation!

In this activity, we will be making simplified "shake sticks," inspired by this magical stick from Chile. Before starting to work, however, you will need to organize a toilet tissue and paper towel roll drive, since these cardboard cylinders will be the basis of our percussion instruments. After you have acquired at least one roller for each child, you are ready to begin.

Materials

- toilet tissue or paper towel rolls
- aluminum foil
- masking tape
- colored plastic tape
- markers
- acrylic paints
- acrylic gloss medium
- brushes
- newspaper
- water
- water cups
- birdseed
- tape recorder
- tape of music from a Latin American country that contains various percussion instruments

Activity

1. Play a selection of music, and ask the children to name some of the musical instruments they hear. Hold a discussion about percussion instruments.

2. Show a "shake stick" you have created at home and demonstrate its sound.

3. Explain to children the general procedure for making this instrument:

   a. Select a toilet tissue or paper towel cardboard roll, and place a small piece of aluminum foil over one end, securing it with masking tape. Layer the tape in several directions over the end of the cylinder, and carefully fasten it to the sides of the cardboard roll.

   b. Next, dump a small amount of birdseed into the roll, and seal the open end with foil and masking tape, as you did the other end.

   c. When the ends have been secured, tape the entire roll using masking tape. Then, try it out for sound!

   d. Next, decorate the taped roll using colored tape, markers, and acrylic paint. Use a variety of pictures and designs.

   e. Finally, the entire roll can be lightly coated with gloss media to seal the designs and tape.

   f. When the creation is dry, the music can begin!

4. Hold a question-and-answer session with the children, and then distribute the materials and let them get to work.

5. When the sticks are ready, the students can pretend they are in a percussion band and shake along to a Spanish or Mexican song.

Follow-Up

Ask the children to write reports on various percussion instruments. Hold an exhibit of the shake sticks, and invite another class to hear a "shake-stick" concert performed by your students.

Helpful Books

- Foster, Karen. *Rattles, Bells, and Chiming Bars.* Brookfield, CT: The Millbrook Press, 1992.
- Mason, Bernard S. *How to Make Drums, Tomtoms & Rattles.* New York: Dover Publications, Inc., 1974.
- Wiseman, Ann. *Making Musical Things.* New York: Charles Scribner's Sons, 1979.

THE BIGGEST TORTILLA

Tortillas are thin cakes of baked cornmeal that can be used to enfold many tasty items. They are popular in Mexico, among other countries, and are lots of fun to eat. In this activity, we will not only sample some tortillas, but we will draw our own version of the largest tortilla.

The prime ingredient for this activity is imagination! So let's imagine for a few moments what the biggest tortilla would look like. How would such a tortilla be prepared? How would it be baked? Would it be used to serve a village or to cover it like a sunshade? Try to stretch your imagination.

Materials

- tortillas
- paper plates
- napkins
- 9" x 12" manila paper
- pencils
- crayons

Activity

1. Begin this activity by discussing tortillas and how they are made.

2. Next, distribute the paper plates and napkins, and let the children sample tortillas. (If you are not sure where to purchase tortillas, keep in mind that some supermarkets sell them in their dairy sections.) How do they taste? What can be served with tortillas?

3. After the sampling is complete, tell the children that in a few minutes, we will be drawing our own version of the biggest tortilla. Tell children the first step is to imagine what such a thing would look like. (You might want to ask the class some of the questions listed in the introduction.)

4. When the children have had an opportunity to brainstorm, distribute the manila paper, pencils, and crayons, and let them begin to draw and color their ideas.

5. After the drawings are finished, hold a sharing session and exhibition.

Follow-Up

Ask the children to write an interesting story to accompany their drawing. Invite a parent or someone you know to class to explain and demonstrate making tortillas.

Helpful Books

- Christian, Rebecca. *Cooking the Spanish Way.* Minneapolis: Lerner Publications, 1982.
- Gomez, Paolo. *Food in Mexico.* Vero Beach, FL: Rourke Publications, 1989.
- Ortiz, Elisabeth Lambert. *Mexican Cooking.* New York: M. Evans and Company, 1967.

FIESTA

Everyone loves a party! Let's imagine for a moment that your classroom is suddenly transformed into the public square of a small village in Spain, Puerto Rico, Mexico, or a country in Central or South America. The important thing is that we have a large public space and we're getting ready to hold a great festival.

A variety of exciting materials and foods should be included in your plans. It is also very important to get the approval of the principal and to enlist the help of class parents; be sure to send information home, with lots of lead time, to obtain specific parental commitments for foods and paper goods. Music is an integral part of any fiesta. Try to gather a variety of tapes or CDs before fiesta day.

Materials

- decorations (such as streamers, piñatas, drawings, and paintings)
- tape
- foods (such as tacos, tortillas, salsa, and the like)
- beverages
- paper plates
- cups
- napkins
- tape recorder or CD player
- variety of music from Spain, Mexico, or a Latin American country

Activity

1. Several weeks before the event, have the children create and send out decorated invitations inviting their parents to the class fiesta.

2. On the day prior to the fiesta, arrange the classroom so that you have a large open central space and desks and chairs at the periphery.

3. Help the children hang piñatas and put up crepe paper streamers and pictures.

4. On fiesta day, coordinate the food and music, and encourage the children to be good hosts and hostesses to the parental visitors.

5. Enjoy the day!

Follow-Up

Ask the children to write a composition about the fiesta. What did they enjoy about it? Have them send thank-you notes to the parents who helped.

Helpful Books

- Martin, Kady. *Let's Party*. Arvada, CO: Cam Co. Publishers, 1986.
- Pals, Ellen M. *Create A Celebration*. Littleton, CO: Aladdin Publishing, 1990.

GAMES

Almost everyone likes to play games! Some games, however, are more interesting and informative than others. The game that we are about to devise is one of the former. The object of the game is to learn the correct Spanish words for some common objects. As part of creating the game, we will be illustrating the objects we wish to identify in Spanish. If you are not familiar with the Spanish language, this activity should be a fine introduction.

Children seem to have a special affinity for picking up a new language. You'll probably witness significant gains in language learning among your students. Before starting this activity, be sure to find out whether anyone in the class speaks Spanish. These children can be a wonderful resource in helping others. It is also very important to make up a large list of common objects, written in Spanish, prior to starting the lesson. You can use a Spanish-English dictionary for this purpose.

Materials

- a large list of common objects written in Spanish
- 3" x 5" cards (unlined)
- 9" x 12" newsprint paper
- pencils
- crayons
- markers

Activity

1. Introduce this topic by asking the children about games. What are some common board games that you play? What do you like about them? Do they contain any artwork or illustrations?

2. Explain that we will be devising a simple game based on learning the Spanish language. How many of you can speak Spanish or know some Spanish words?

3. Tell the children that you will be distributing copies of a Spanish word list in a few minutes and will be asking each child to choose any five words on the list. He/she should carefully write those

words in Spanish and English on the paper provided, and make some simple sketches to illustrate the words selected.

4. Pass out the word list, the newsprint paper, and the pencils, and let the children begin their word search and preliminary sketches.

5. When everyone has completed this portion of the activity, distribute the 3" x 5" cards, crayons and markers, and ask each child to carefully print one Spanish word on one side of each card and then to make an illustration of this word on the opposite side.

6. When everyone has finished, collect all the cards and look them over. Then, have the class divide up into small groups (2 to 4 children per group), and give each group 10 to 20 cards with which to work. Have the students begin to learn the words by associating them with the pictures.

7. Eventually, the children should be able to give the correct Spanish word for each picture shown. A sample word list follows:

mother - madre	**house** - casa	**television** - televisión
girl - muchacha	**door** - puerta	**dress** - vestido
father - padre	**school** - escuela	**telephone** - teléfono
teacher - maestra	**window** - ventana	**pants** - pantalónes
sister - hermana	**apartment** - apartamento	**radio** - radio
student - estudiante		**shoes** - zapatos
brother - hermano	**book** - libro	**picture** - pintura
cat - gato	**table** - mesa	**tree** - árbol
boy - muchacho	**hat** - sombrero	
dog - perro	**chair** - silla	
	coat - saco	

Follow-Up

Practice makes perfect! During periods of free time, encourage the children to practice their Spanish using these picture-cards.

Helpful Books

- Editors of Passport Books. *Let's Learn Spanish Picture Dictionary.* Lincolnwood, IL: Passport Books, 1993.
- Nardelli, Robert R. *Dictionary in Spanish* (The Cat in the Hat Beginner Book.) New York: Random House, Inc., 1966.

117

MOLAS

Molas are special embroidered cloth collages created by the Cuna Indians of Panama. Because of their wonderful designs, they have become one of Panama's most important forms of art. The themes for most molas are birds, animals, and plant life; colors are usually bright and striking. Although the Panamanians originally created molas as wall decorations, in more recent times, these fabric pictures often appear on vests and shirts.

In this activity, we will be designing and creating our own molas. Your subject matter does not have to be the traditional parrot, toucan, or palm tree. It can be a rendition of your dog or cat, or the big maple tree down the block. In other words, you can select a subject, if you wish, that is nearby rather than one from Panama!

Since real molas require cloth and sewing, we will be making simplified versions using paper and glue. Before starting this activity with your class, try to get some actual molas or pictures of them to show to the children.

Materials

- 9" x 12" manila paper
- 9" x 12" colored construction paper
- tissue paper
- crepe paper
- paper scraps
- pencils
- markers
- white glue
- scissors

Activity

1. Introduce the topic of molas, and discuss this form of art. Show some pictures or actual molas to the class, and explain how they are made.

2. Tell the class that we will soon be making our own molas out of construction paper, tissue, and crepe paper. Ask each child to think of a theme for his/her mola, and distribute the manila paper and pencils so that students can sketch their ideas.

3. When the children have selected the individual themes they like best, distribute the rest of the materials, and ask the children to transfer their sketches to the colored construction paper. It's a good idea to choose a single background color from the construction paper assortment, then glue the rest of your design to it. Stitch marks can be added by using the markers.

4. When the molas are finished, hold a sharing session and exhibit.

Follow-Up

A quick study of Panama and some of the other countries in Central America might be interesting. The children could do some research, either individually or in groups, and report back to the class about this area of the world.

Helpful Books

• Haynes, Tricia. *Let's Visit Panama.* London: Burke Publishing Company, Ltd., 1984.

Families—

A special group of people,
They make us feel great.

With relatives and dogs and things,
They keep us running straight.

They cheer us when we're feeling low,
They give our lives a special glow.

Whether they are big or small,
Having a family is really a ball!

Families help to make our lives worthwhile and meaningful. Indeed, the special support and opportunities for sharing that families provide enable each of us to grow and develop to the fullest. Although family life is not always perfect, having a truly loving and supportive family is a wonderful thing.

Families come in many sizes and configurations. Sometimes there are two parents, and sometimes one parent. Sometimes the two parents are of different sexes, and sometimes they're of the same sex. Some families have lots of children, aunts, uncles, grandparents, and even great grandparents, while other families have very few relatives. Some of us have been born into a family, and some of us have been chosen to be family members. The key word about families is "variety," and that's what makes them so interesting!

During Family History Month, we will be thinking about our families and doing a number of activities to better understand and celebrate them. We will be depicting a family figure, interviewing an older member of our family, and relating a family story—one, perhaps, from the distant past or one from more recent times. We will also be designing our own family tree, doing a portrait of someone in our family, and creating a family crest.

The people we include in these activities may live nearby or at a great distance; some may no longer be alive. The important thing is that they're linked to us by a special bond. October's activities will help us explore this bond and give lots of insights into some very special people indeed—the members of our family.

A FAMILY FIGURE

Different members of our family influence us in different ways. It could be a personality trait, the way they tell a joke, or a smile or laugh that we remember. Perhaps they have a special way of encouraging us, or standing by us when we need help. Maybe they take us fishing, or bake wonderful cookies for us, or are really good at discussing problems. Whatever their special talents, people in our families definitely touch our lives in all kinds of ways!

In this activity, we will be selecting a family member and depicting him or her in a montage. Before starting this activity, collect a variety of old magazines for your students' use.

Materials

- composition paper
- 12" x 18" colored posterboard
- magazines
- manila folders
- crayons
- markers
- scissors
- white glue

Activity

1. Start this activity by launching a class discussion about family members. Ask the children to carefully consider the different people in their families and to name some of the qualities that these people possess.

2. List some of the children's responses on the chalkboard. Be sure to point out that there are many different things that we notice about the people in our families.

121

3. Next, ask each child to select one family member and to create a montage about that person. Explain that a montage is a collection of pictures and words, arranged and glued in an artistic way.

4. Before starting the artwork, distribute the composition paper, and ask each child to list some of the key qualities of the person he/she selected. Then, dispense the rest of the materials, and let the children begin to work on their montages.

5. When the works are complete, hold a sharing session and exhibit.

Follow-Up

Invite each child to write a short composition or poem about her/his family figure.

Helpful Books

- Boyd, Lizi. *The Not-So-Wicked Stepmother.* New York: Viking Kestrel, 1987.
- Cole, Joanna. *The New Baby at Your House.* New York: William Morrow and Company, Inc., 1985.
- Harranth, Wolf. *My Old Grandad.* Oxford: Oxford University Press, 1984.
- Simon, Norma. *All Kinds of Families.* Niles, IL: Albert Whitman, 1976.

INTERVIEWING AN OLDER RELATIVE

Some people have a marvelous talent for telling fascinating stories about past events. In our family, we are lucky to have both my mother, Louise Ryder, and my mother-in-law, Constance Siegel, who possess this special gift. Thanks to them, we have gained a great many insights into our family history. Without their stories, we would know very little indeed about how our relatives—both in Europe and America—lived, and what their lives were like.

Most of us know only small bits and pieces of our family history. This activity is designed to change all that! We will be interviewing an older relative and listening to some stories we may never before have heard about our families. In doing so, we may come to appreciate our families all the more.

The ability to ask simple, open-ended questions, and to listen very carefully to the answers are important components of this activity. A cassette tape recorder is a great thing to use when interviewing your relative. If this equipment isn't available, try to take some brief notes as the person answers your questions.

Before introducing this activity to your class, interview one of your own relatives, and tape or jot down some of his/her stories.

Materials

- notebook or composition paper
- pencils
- pens
- cassette tape recorder (if available)
- blank tape

Activity

1. Introduce this activity by playing a tape of one of your relatives telling a story, or by briefly relating such a story through your notes.

123

2. Explain that in this activity, we will be interviewing one of our older relatives in order to gain a better understanding of our family history.

3. Ask the children to choose the person they wish to interview, and to formulate some questions that they would like to ask that person. You may wish to pass out a list of suggested questions, such as the one that follows, to further assist your students.

   • What were things like when you were a kid?
   • Can you tell me about some funny incidents from your past?
   • What do you remember about another country or city?
   • Where did you live as a child?
   • What was the climate like?
   • What was your house or apartment like?
   • What kind of family gatherings did you attend?
   • What pets did you have?
   • How were holidays celebrated?
   • What kind of games did you play?
   • How did you meet another relative (ask, for example, how your mother met your father)?
   • What was school like?

4. After everyone has their questions prepared, remind them to bring a tape recorder and blank tape, or a notebook and pen/pencil to their interview.

5. Assign a certain date by which the children should have conducted their interview.

6. When all the interviews are complete, hold a sharing session and story hour.

Follow-Up

Invite the interviewees to attend a special "Meet the Relatives Class Party." Ask each child to make a drawing based on something he/she learned about the family.

Helpful Books

• Harranth, Wolf. *My Old Grandad.* Oxford: Oxford University Press, 1984.
• Khalsa, Dayal Kaur. *Tales of a Gambling Grandma.* New York: Clarkson N. Potter, Inc., 1986.
• LeShan, Eda. *Grandparents: A Special Kind of Love.* New York: Macmillan, 1984.
• Simon, Norma. *All Kinds of Families.* Niles, IL: Albert Whitman, 1976.

124

TELLING A FAMILY STORY

The words "humorous," "unusual," and "amazing" are a few of the adjectives that may spring to mind when someone tells a family story. The idea behind this activity is having each child relate a truly special story to the class. Although the story could be based on an event from the distant past, it might be more interesting for each child to tell a story from her/his own experience.

When my daughter, Tama, was about 10 years old, she wrote a family story for school. The theme was one of the "smoky barbecues" for which I am well-known in my neighborhood. This particular barbecue nearly succeeded in bringing out the local fire department and certainly brought my neighbor running to the back of my house, a bucket of water in hand, fearing that my roof was on fire! As you might imagine, this little tale has improved with each telling over the years.

Begin this activity by coming up with a fine family story of your own to tell your students. This should help set the tone and serve as a wonderful motivator for your class.

Materials

- composition paper
- pencils
- pens
- 9" x 12" manila paper
- crayons

Activity

1. Introduce this topic by telling a family story of your own. Try to keep all stories, including your own, as brief as possible.

2. When you have completed your tale, explain that each of us will be telling our own family story. You might remind the children, that their parents may not wish them to share certain stories with the class.

125

3. Before doing any story-telling, distribute the composition paper, pencils, and pens, and ask each child to come up with a story and jot it down in rough form on composition paper. Consider setting a 15-minute time limit on this portion of the activity.

4. When the compositions are finished, gather the children in a large circle, and invite them to tell their stories. They needn't read directly from their papers, but may wish to use them for reference.

5. When the storytelling is completed, have the children rewrite their compositions, and make crayon drawings on manila paper to illustrate them.

6. Display the family stories and drawings in the classroom or hallway.

Follow-Up

Invite the parents of your students to share in a "Retelling Session" of the family stories.

Helpful Books

- Cole, Joanna. *The New Baby at Your House.* New York: William Morrow and Company, Inc., 1985.
- Drescher, Joan. *My Mother's Getting Married.* New York: Dial Books for Young Readers, 1986.
- Hazen, Barbara Shook. *Two Homes to Live In.* New York: Human Sciences Press, 1978.
- Livingston, Carole. *Why Was I Adopted?* Secaucus, NJ: Lyle Stuart Inc., 1978.
- Powledge, Fred. *So You're Adopted.* New York: Charles Scribner's Sons, 1982.
- Tax, Meredith. *Families.* Boston: Little, Brown, 1981.

DESIGNING A FAMILY TREE

All of us have relatives. Our relatives may be biologically related to us, or related to us by marriage. Some of us have been specially selected (adopted) into a family, which is a wonderful thing. Whatever our situation, we are related to somebody else!

In this activity, we will be thinking about our relatives and representing them in a family tree. Although some family trees are complicated, we shall try to keep ours simple and direct.

Before "embarking" on this subject with your class, prepare a family tree of your own. Then introduce the idea to your class, and let them "branch" out on it! Everyone will "root" for this subject, once they get started.

Materials

- 9" x 12" manila paper
- 12" x 18" colored construction paper
- paper scraps
- pencils
- markers
- rulers
- scissors
- white glue

Activity

1. Begin this activity by discussing what a family tree is. Explain that a family tree shows us who we are related to. In this activity, we will be designing simple family trees that include some of our relatives.

2. Show your family tree to the students, and let them ask questions about it. Be sure to mention that the trunk, branches, and leaves

127

can be made in any style they wish, whether abstract, realistic, primitive, etc.

3. Next, describe the general procedure for making a family tree

   a. First, draw the trunk of the tree and write in your last name. Keep the lettering as neat as possible by using light pencil guidelines.

   b. Now, draw a branch for each family member you wish to include on your tree and write in his/her name. Add new branches as you think of more family members.

   c. Then, at the end of each branch, where the leaves would be, include a special symbol representing him/her. For example, if your grandfather smokes a pipe, a drawing of a pipe might be added. A photo of the person might also be used.

4. Once the children understand these concepts, they're ready to begin. Distribute the 9" x 12" manila paper, so that rough sketches of the family trees can be made.

5. After each child has finished his/her sketch, distribute the other materials. Have the students do enlarged versions of their sketches using cut paper. Everyone should select one piece of 12" x 18" colored construction paper as a background, and cut and glue the other pieces—trunk, branches, leaves, fruits, and the like—to it.

6. When all the trees are in full bloom, hold a sharing session and exhibit.

Follow-Up

Ask each child to invite one of his/her family tree members to class for a small get-together. The kids can show their trees to their relatives, while sharing some goodies with them.

Helpful Books

- Lewis, Helen Coale. *All About Families: The Second Time Around.* Atlanta, GA: Peachtree Publishers, 1980.
- Meltzer, Milton. *A Book About Names.* New York: Thomas Y. Crowell, 1984.
- Perl, Lila. *The Great Ancestor Hunt.* New York: Clarion Books, 1989.
- Stryker-Rodda, Harriet. *How to Climb Your Family Tree.* Philadelphia: J. B. Lippincott, 1977.

PORTRAITS OF A FAMILY MEMBER

Have you ever looked closely at someone in your family while he or she was reading, watching television, or doing a household chore? If your family includes pets, have you ever studied your dog or cat as it rested in your house? People and animals are loaded with interesting qualities and distinct physical characteristics. In this activity, we will try to capture some of these things by sketching a portrait of a member of our family—be it person or pet.

Before introducing the activity in class, try it on your own. This way, you'll know exactly what's involved in doing a charcoal portrait. You may also wish to do a little art history research at the library, and bring in portraits by various artists to show the class.

Materials

- 9" x 12" and 12" x 18" newsprint paper
- pencils
- vine charcoal
- newspaper
- tissues

Activity

1. Introduce the idea of creating a portrait of a family member by showing students the work you did at home, and/or by showing them the portraits you located.

2. Explain that in this activity, each of us will be asked to select a member of the family as the subject of a portrait. Remember to remind the class that pets can also count. When the children get home, but before they begin any drawing, ask them to carefully study the person or pet they selected. Encourage them to notice

129

From *Celebrating Diversity with Art: Thematic Projects for Every Month of the Year*, published by GoodYearBooks. Copyright © 1995 by Willet Ryder.

the most outstanding features of the person or animal—for example, large mustache, long whiskers, wrinkles, particular hair style, and the like.

3. Then, using the 9" x 12" newsprint paper and pencils, the children should make a few pencil sketches of their subject, and bring these to class.

4. After the pencil drawings have been brought to class, explain that we will be using the sketches to make charcoal portraits. Be sure to mention that charcoal is fun, but it can be messy! Show students how to apply charcoal and how to blend it using a finger or tissue.

5. Then, dispense the newspaper (for covering the desks), the 12" x 18" newsprint paper, the vine charcoal, and some tissues. Invite each child to carefully enlarge his/her portrait using the charcoal. Remind the children that the style of their drawings is up to them.

6. When the portraits are complete, set up a portrait gallery in your classroom or hallway.

Follow-Up

Invite the "people subjects" to a gallery opening to see their portraits. Serve some goodies to enhance the event, if you like.

Helpful Books

- Simon, Norma. *All Kinds of Families.* Niles, IL: Albert Whitman, 1976.
- Tax, Meredith. *Families.* Boston: Little, Brown, 1981.

A FAMILY CREST

Designing a family crest or heraldic symbol can be an exciting experience. Some families already have a crest or symbol that represents their name; others do not. In this activity, we will be designing our own family crests.

A family crest is an ancient art form that extends back to the Middle Ages in Europe. Special crests and symbols were used to identify royal officials and important persons in many parts of the world even before that time period. In Asia, for example, Japan utilized a unique form of heraldry.

In designing a crest, it's a good idea to begin with one's interests or with symbols that have strong personal meaning. If one enjoys growing tulips, for example, these might make a fine design motif for a crest.

Before starting this activity with the class, take time to work on your own family crest at home. In addition, make a trip to your local library and gather some books or posters on the subject (look under "Heraldry" and "Coats of Arms"). After you have assembled these materials, you are ready to introduce the activity in class.

Materials

- 9" x 12" manila and white drawing paper
- pencils
- colored pencils
- markers
- rulers
- watercolors
- small brushes
- water cups
- water
- newspaper
- paper towels

Activity

1. Show the children the books you gathered and display the family crest you designed. Answer any questions the children may have.

2. Explain that each of us will be designing our own family crest. Give a short history of family crests. Point out that since many of us may not have a symbol or coat of arms for our family, we can invent one by using our own interests as a starting point. We can also make one by literally translating our name and depicting it.

3. Distribute the 9" x 12" manila paper and pencils, and ask the children to make some sketches. Although shield shapes were often used to contain designs in the Middle Ages, any shape can be created and used.

4. Invite each child to choose his/her favorite design, and carefully transfer it to the white drawing paper. The designs can be colored using colored pencils, markers, and watercolors. Remind the children to use light pencil guidelines when lettering their names so that the letters are clear and uniform.

5. When all the family crests are complete, hold a sharing session and exhibit.

Follow-Up

If you photocopy the family crests, these can serve as neat bookcovers for individual works containing small photographs and selected information about each student's family.

Helpful Books

- Fradon, Dana. *Harold the Herald*. New York: Dutton Children's Books, 1990.
- Perl, Lila. *The Great Ancestor Hunt*. New York: Clarion Books, 1989.
- Ryder, Willet. *The Art Experience*. Glenview, IL: GoodYearBooks, 1991.

The sand was soft under our tent, and the night sky was filled with a thousand stars. Huge rocky sentinels and high mesas guarded the mysterious desert lands. The place was Navajo country—Kayenta, Arizona—and we, visitors here, felt happy and honored to be camping on a part of the Navajo Reservation. I have always been interested in the amazing history and culture of Native Americans, and this trip was one of many, that I have taken to learn more about America's first people.

Today, Native Americans live in various regions of the United States. The tribes and nations of the Southwest are among the best known—especially for their magnificent art. It is from this area that Zuni fetishes, Pueblo pottery, and Navajo turquoise jewelry originate. Yet other parts of the country are home to Native Americans with famous names and achievements of their own, the Algonquin, the Cherokee, the Iroquois, and the Sioux, to name a few. The list is long and tinged with sadness for the Native Americans who have suffered so much at the hands of white settlers.

During this month, we will try to gain a clearer understanding of the original "Americans" and learn something of their wisdom. We will make drums and do some dancing. We will learn about Native American games and toys. We will explore the Native American view on nature and land, and we will study corn. We will also do some beadwork, and create a petroglyph. In short, we will sample just a few of the many cultural contributions we owe to these amazing people.

DRUMS AND DANCES

Drumbeats are heard from every corner of the globe, yet Native Americans are uniquely associated with drums and tom-toms. The drum, a percussion instrument, is used to establish special rhythms connected with religious and sacred rituals. Anyone who has ever witnessed a ceremonial dance can appreciate the significance of the drum.

Drums have a special place in Native American ceremonies and traditions. Not only do they vary in terms of size and shape, but the decoration of these instruments marks the cultural variety and creativity of their makers. Often used to celebrate natural events, drums are sometimes decorated with symbols associated with the forces of nature. Feathers and fur trappings may be added, giving these instruments a special character.

In this activity, we will be making drums and choreographing some simple dances. Since the traditional process of stretching skins over wood or metal frames to make drums is too complicated, we will be substituting contemporary containers to save us time. Before starting this activity with your class, hold a can and container drive so that every child will be guaranteed an instrument. It's important to make sure that the cans and containers collected also have their own plastic covers or tops. The following cans and containers work well: bread crumb, coffee, peanut, and oatmeal. Make a point of visiting your local library, prior to the activity, to get a tape or CD of Native American songs and music.

Materials

- assorted cans and containers with covers
- colored construction paper and paper scraps
- scissors
- rulers
- pencils
- white glue
- masking tape
- yarn
- feathers
- found objects
- markers
- tape player or CD player
- tape or CD of Native American music

Activity

1. Introduce the concept of Native American drums to your students by playing a tape and/or showing a drum you have made at home.

2. Discuss how drums are used in Native American culture, listing some of the possible occasions on the chalkboard. Celebrations might honor birth, marriage, death, harvest, war, corn, rain, and sun.

3. Explain that each child will be decorating her/his own drum, using the cans and containers we have collected. Before distributing these materials, discuss and illustrate some symbols that the children might use as decorative motifs. Examples include lightning, snakes, the sun, stars, and the like.

4. Next, show students how to cover the outside of the container or can using construction paper and glue. Explain that the paper can be measured to fit the side, glue can be applied, and then the paper rolled around the can. The ends can be temporarily fixed with masking tape, until the glue has dried.

5. Distribute the materials, and let the children begin to work. When the cans are covered, decorations can be made of construction paper, and glued to the sides of the cans, and markers used for further embellishment, Yarn, feathers, and found objects can be added to create additional interest.

6. When the drums have been completed, try them out for sound.

7. Then, divide the class into small groups, and have each group research and develop a short, simple dance based on an important event.

8. Hold a class drum-and-dance session.

Follow-Up

Invite another class in to see your class perform. The children might also research and create some simple clothing to enhance their dances.

Helpful Books

- Fichter, George S. *American Indian Music and Musical Instruments.* New York: David McKay, 1978.

- Hofsinde, Robert (Gray-Wolf). *Indian Music Makers.* New York: William Morrow, 1967.

- McGrath, James. *Dance with Indian Children.* Santa Fe, NM: Institute of American Indian Arts, 1970-71.

- McGrath, James. *My Music Reaches to the Sky.* Santa Fe, NM: Indian America Design Workshop, 1971.

- Paker, Josephine. *Beating the Drum.* Brookfield, CT: The Millbrook Press, 1992.

GAMES AND TOYS

Everyone enjoys games and toys! In this activity, we will be researching some Native American games and toys. Perhaps one of the most famous of these is "stickball," which we know as "lacrosse." What others can you discover? To aid the children in their research, it might be helpful to provide them with a list of some Native American peoples. A short sample list follows: Algonquin, Apache, Arapaho, Cherokee, Comanche, Haida, Hopi, Iroquois, Natchez, Navajo, Onondaga, Pawnee, Sioux, Zuni. Encourage the children to use the list as a way to organize their investigation of Native American games and pastimes.

Materials

- composition paper
- 9" x 12" manila paper
- pencils
- crayons
- markers

Activity

1. Ask the children in your class to tell you the names of some of the games and toys that they enjoy. Make a list of their answers on the chalkboard.

2. Explain that all people enjoy games and toys, and that Native Americans are no exception. Point out that in this activity, each child or group of children will be asked to research a Native American game or toy and tell the class about it.

3. Provide the children with a sample list of Native American peoples. Then bring them to the school library to do some research.

4. Ask each child or small group to take notes on a Native American game or toy and write a short composition about it.

5. In addition, invite each child or group to create an illustration of the game or toy selected, using the manila paper, crayons, and markers.

6. Hold a sharing session and exhibit the children's work.

Follow-Up

Select a few games and help the children learn how to play them.

Helpful Books

- Blood, Charles L. *American Indian Games and Crafts.* New York: Franklin Watts, 1981.
- Gogniat, Maurice. *Indian Toys You Can Make.* New York: Sterling Publishing, 1976.
- Purdy, Susan and Sandak, Cass R. *North American Indians.* New York: Franklin Watts, 1982.

FITTING INTO NATURE

According to Native American philosophy, the person is a part of the land—that is, a guardian and extension of nature. Although we are all part of the natural world, our modern technology and thinking have often worked to set us apart, severing our connection to natural things. The Native American view leads to a refreshing rediscovery of our primal roots.

It is with these thoughts in mind that we approach this next activity. Native Americans have traditionally made a supreme effort to try to fit into nature, rather than conquer it. How have the first residents of the Americas accomplished this mission? What practices have they employed? What is their view on land, water, and nature, in general?

In this activity, we will try to find the answers to these questions, as we paint some landscapes that depict the special position of nature in Native American life.

It's a good idea to do some of your own library research on this topic before introducing it to your class. Make a visit to the library, locate some books on Native American culture, and bring them to class. You might also wish to bring in some books featuring pictures of landscapes from different parts of this country.

Materials	• 9" x 12" manila and white drawing paper	• water cups
	• pencil	• water
	• crayons	• paper towels
	• watercolors	• newspapers
	• brushes	

139

Activity

1. Write the following questions on the chalkboard: How do Native Americans view nature and the land? Is their view different from that of other people? Explain that we will try to answer these questions. In doing so, we will attempt to understand why and how Native Americans see themselves as part of nature.

2. Hold a discussion on this topic, and distribute some of the books you have collected.

3. Ask the children to go to the school library to find other books on the subject. In addition, ask them to find pictures of landscapes, from any section of the country, which will serve as the basis for watercolor paintings.

4. Ideally, each child should select a different picture. Point out that the painting need not look exactly like the original.

5. After the children have selected their pictures, ask them to make a sketch of it on the manila paper.

6. When the sketches are complete, they should be transferred to the white drawing paper using pencils and/or crayons, and painted with watercolors. Don't forget to encourage students' use of various artistic styles!

7. The finished paintings should be discussed, and then displayed in the classroom or hallway.

Follow-Up

Ask the children to write a short composition or poem about the Native American viewpoint on nature, and why it is important for us to know about it.

Helpful Books

- Billard, Jules B., editor. *The World of the American Indian.* Washington, DC: The National Geographic Society, 1979.
- Gibson, Michael R. *The North American Indian.* London: Theorem Publishing Ltd., 1978.
- Liptak, Karen. *North American Indian Survival Skills.* New York: Franklin Watts, 1990.
- White, Anne Terry (from text by William Brandon). *The American Indian.* New York: Random House, 1963.
- Wood, Marion. *Ancient America.* New York: Facts On File, 1990.

POPCORN AND CORNBREAD

There's more than a "kernel" of truth to the story that Native Americans introduced the settlers from Europe to the remarkable potentials of corn! This wonderful vegetable was used by America's original inhabitants in a variety of ways. It was popped, boiled, roasted, and ground. It was served at regular meals, as well as at sacred festivals and dances. The special qualities of corn, among them resilience, allowed it to be stored and transported around the country.

Many of us know corn best through attending the movies, and munching on popcorn. Although this tasty snack is great with salt and melted butter, it can also be eaten like a breakfast cereal, with milk and sugar. Cornbread is another tasty treat (a number of recipes can still be found for this hearty bread on boxes of cornmeal in your local supermarket). Well, enough of these "corny" stories, let's get on with the activity.

In this activity, we will be focusing on corn and sampling it in a couple of forms. We will also be studying the vegetable itself, and making drawings of it. Before introducing this topic to your class, pick up several ears of corn at your local supermarket or farm stand. In addition, purchase or prepare some popcorn and cornbread, and bring all these items to school, along with some napkins and paper plates.

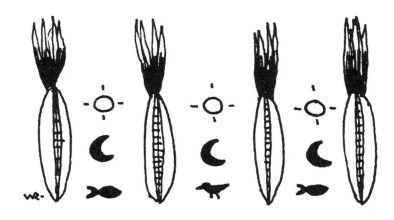

Materials

- several ears of corn
- popcorn
- cornbread
- paper plates
- napkins
- 9" x 12" manila paper
- pencils
- crayons
- markers

Activity

1. Ask the children if they have ever eaten corn. What form was the corn in (for example, popped, boiled, etc.)? Make a list on the chalkboard of some of the creations that contain corn. These include popcorn, cornbread, cereal, and tortillas.

2. Explain that we will be sampling two different corn creations, namely popcorn and cornbread. Point out to the children that we owe our knowledge of this vegetable to Native Americans.

3. Distribute the paper goods, popcorn and cornbread, and let the sampling begin!

4. After the children finish snacking, and clearing the plates, tell them that we will be making a drawing of some ears of corn using pencils, crayons, and markers.

5. Next, show the children the ears of corn, and display them in the front of the room or on a table in the center of the room. Dispense the manila paper, pencils, crayons, and markers, and let the children begin to draw.

6. Remind the children to carefully study the corn as they're drawing it. They may also want to make abstract corn designs based on what they see.

7. When the drawings are complete, hold a discussion and "corny" art exhibit.

Follow-Up

Ask the kids to investigate this vegetable further and to write a "corny" story!

Helpful Books

- de Paola, Tomie. *The Popcorn Book.* New York: Holiday House, 1978.
- Hays, Wilma P. and R. Vernon. *Foods the Indians Gave Us.* New York: Ives Washburn, 1973.
- Lavine, Sigmund A. *Indian Corn and Other Gifts.* New York: Dodd, Mead, 1974.
- Purdy, Susan and Sandak, Cass R. *North American Indians.* New York: Franklin Watts, 1982.

BEADWORK

When I was a child, my family had a pair of old deerskin moccasins with some beautiful beadwork on them. They were kept in a large attic trunk, which looked like an ancient treasure chest. Although I liked wearing the moccasins, I also enjoyed just looking at them and admiring their elaborate beaded designs.

Beads have always played an important role in Native American culture. They were used as both an element of beautification and a medium of exchange. Beads come in a variety of materials, styles, and colors. On Long Island, tiny shells known as wampum were used as money.

In this activity, we will be using a selection of beads to create a simple bracelet or necklace. To carry out the work with your class, you will need a variety of beads and other supplies. Therefore, a trip to a local bead dealer, floral supply house, or craft store is a good idea before you introduce the activity. A variety of uncooked pasta can also be utilized as beads.

In addition, check your local library for books with pictures of Native American beadwork. You should also make your own beaded bracelet or necklace at home, before launching the activity at school.

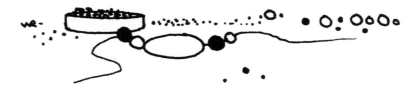

Materials

- a variety of beads and uncooked pasta
- yarn
- thin leather cord
- heavy thread
- scissors
- small jeweler's pliers
- assorted jewelry elements (hooks & eyes, spring clips & rings)

Activity

1. Introduce this activity by showing some pictures of Native American beadwork. Explain the importance of beads in Native American culture, and show the sample bracelet or necklace that you created.

2. Mention to the class that beads come in many types, sizes, shapes, and colors. Some beads are very expensive, while others are quite affordable. Explain to the class that each child will be making his/her own beaded bracelet or necklace.

3. Briefly describe the technique of stringing beads, and stress the fact that each jewelry design should be different. Encourage the kids to experiment with their designs when they begin working with the materials.

4. Allow the children to select a number of beads from the supply you brought to class, and give each child a section of cord and a pair of scissors. Then, let everyone get to work.

5. Circulate through the classroom, giving individual guidance to each child about his/her design as needed. Remind students that to hold the beads in a fixed position, knots must be tied in the cord.

6. If the children wish to use findings, such as clips and rings, you can assist them in attaching these items. (In some cases, a pair of jeweler's pliers may be needed.)

7. When the bracelets and necklaces are complete, hold a discussion and exhibit the work in the school showcase.

Follow-Up

Ask the children to do research on the topic of beadwork, and have them write a composition about this art form. You may want to display the compositions alongside the jewelry.

Helpful Books

- Aikman, Z. Susanne. A Primer: *The Art of Native American Beadwork.* Denver, CO: Morning Flower Press, 1980.
- Blood, Charles L. *American Indian Games and Crafts.* New York: Franklin Watts, 1981.
- Hofsinde, Robert (Gray-Wolf). *Indian Beadwork.* New York: William Morrow, 1958.

PETROGLYPHS IN PLASTER

Several years ago, my wife and I went hiking through Petroglyph National Park outside Albuquerque, New Mexico. Although we watched closely for rattlesnakes, we primarily concentrated on the amazing rock etchings that the ancient Pueblo peoples created in this area. The varied symbols depicted hands, figures, animals, and natural forces, among other things.

Petroglyphs occur in many areas of the world, and are mysterious to study and contemplate. They represent the desire of ancient peoples to leave tangible and significant marks about their existence and life-styles. Although the Native Americans of the past used sharp stones to incise designs in larger rocks, we will be using our fingers and sticks to create designs in plaster.

Before starting this activity, it's important to do a little library research on petroglyphs and to make a plaster petroglyph at home. Keep in mind that plaster is a fun, but messy, material! So if you don't enjoy a mess, stay away from this activity.

Materials

- 9" x 12" newsprint paper
- pencils
- plastic or heavy cardboard bowls
- large plastic bucket
- water
- plaster of paris
- assorted sticks
- salad oil
- string
- scissors
- assorted tempera paint
- brushes
- paint cups
- paper towels
- large plastic bags
- newspaper

1. Show the children some pictures or books on petroglyphs, and list the term on the board.

2. Ask the children what they think these rock designs mean and why the ancient Native Americans created them.

3. Discuss some of the symbols that were used in these rock carvings, and draw a few of them on the chalkboard.

4. Distribute the newsprint paper and pencils, and ask each child to make a few sketches for her/his own petroglyph design. Ask each child to set aside his/her favorite design while you demonstrate the following process for making plaster petroglyphs:

   a. First, cover all work surfaces with large plastic bags or newspapers.

   b. Next, fill a large plastic bucket with water to a little over the halfway point. Add plaster of Paris until you form a little island on the top of the water that doesn't sink! Using your hand and forearm, gently stir the plaster into the water, forming a creamy white mixture.

   c. Then, take a heavy plastic or cardboard bowl, and pour a small amount of salad oil into it. Wipe the oil around the inner surface of the bowl using a paper towel.

   d. Now, carefully pour the plaster mixture into the bowl to just above the halfway mark.

   e. Then, cut a piece of string (approximately 6" in length), and insert it into the wet plaster, leaving a loop that extends up the edge of the bowl. This loop will eventually be used for hanging purposes.

   f. Watch carefully as the mixture hardens. Feel the side of the bowl; plaster will actually generate heat during the drying process.

   g. When the mixture looks nearly dry, use your finger or a stick to incise the design from your pencil sketch into the plaster.

   h. After the plaster is completely dry, gently remove the petroglyph from the bowl.

   i. Leave the finished petroglyphs white or paint them to resemble rock, using the tempera paint and brushes.

5. Once the children understand this process, they are ready to begin making their own plaster petroglyphs. You, the teacher, should be the official plaster mixer and pourer.

6. When the petroglyphs are complete, hold a discussion and display.

Follow-Up

Ask the children to do some research on petroglyphs, and write short reports about them. Include these reports in the petroglyph display.

Helpful Books

- Bartok, Mira, and Ronan, Christine. *Pueblo Indians of the Southwest.* Glenview, IL: GoodYearBooks.
- D'Apice, Mary. *The Pueblo.* Vero Beach, FL: Rourke Publications, Inc., 1990.
- Patterson-Rudolph, Carol. *Petroglyphs & Pueblo Myths of the Rio Grande.* Albuquerque, NM: Avanyu Publishing, 1990.
- Schaafsma, Polly. *Indian Rock Art of the Southwest.* Santa Fe, NM: School of American Research, 1980.

By simply flipping through a newspaper or tuning into the news, one encounters problems concerning human rights. Every country around the globe needs to better address issues dealing with human hunger, poverty, equality, and dignity.

Universal Human Rights Month, the last month of the year, is an ideal time to ponder some of the serious problems facing people in our neighborhood and around the world. During this month, we will investigate human rights issues as we take part in a number of thoughtful activities designed to enhance our understanding of ourselves and others.

We will begin by asking some tough questions and present our answers artistically. We will make word designs based on humanistic concepts. We will contemplate some of the many freedoms in the United States, and form sculptures to represent them. We will build symbolic bridges which connect our country to another, as well as create our vision of a better world. Finally, we will lend a helping hand to a fellow traveler on life's exciting journey.

Universal Human Rights Month is filled with both problems and promise! It challenges all of us, both teacher and student, to make things a little better and brighter for people everywhere.

WHAT WOULD YOU DO?

Imagine for a moment that you have been asked to think of a solution to one of the serious problems facing human beings. Let's take hunger, for example. How would you, personally, work on solving this problem? What actions would you take? Where would you begin?

In this activity, we will be taking up a human rights issue and making a drawing suggesting a solution to the problem. The drawing you create can be done in any style which you wish. It could realistically depict a hungry person being given a wonderful meal or abstractly depict the word "food." The focus for this activity is on how each of us would solve a distinct problem. The ways we approach the problem should be as varied as we are.

Before doing this activity with your class, take time to try it yourself at home. The crucial point, of course, is that each person be given the opportunity to really think about a significant human rights issue.

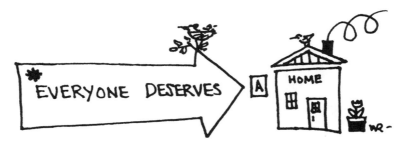

Materials

- 9" x 12" manila paper
- 12" x 18" white drawing paper
- pencils
- crayons
- markers

Activity

1. Introduce this topic by holding a class discussion on some of the many issues related to human rights. What are some of the problems? How could we begin to solve such problems?

2. Make a list on the chalkboard of the issues students suggest. These might include poverty, hunger, homelessness, lack of free speech, war, and religious persecution.

3. Ask each child to select an issue that he/she feels strongly about and to think about creating an artwork, in any style, that represents the issue and a possible solution.

4. Distribute the 9" x 12" manila paper and pencils, and have the students sketch their ideas.

5. When the sketches are complete, pass out the 12" x 18" white drawing paper, crayons, and markers, and invite each student to transfer and enlarge her/his drawing.

6. After the final drawings have been completed, hold a sharing session and exhibit.

Follow-Up

Ask the children to write short reports about the problem and solution they depicted. Exhibit these reports alongside the artworks.

Helpful Books

- Greene, Laura. *Help: Getting to Know about Needing and Giving.* New York: Human Sciences Press, 1981.
- United Nations. *A Children's Chorus.* New York: Dutton, 1989.

ILLUSTRATING WORDS

During Universal Human Rights Month, many special words spring to mind—words such as *care, share, help, friendship, and concern*. In this activity, we will be selecting a word related to human rights, and using it to create a word design. The design will be composed of small repeated copies of the selected word, either written in script or printed.

Before introducing this activity, sit down with your dictionary or thesaurus and compile a list of some important words. You may wish to make copies of the list for each child. Remember to bring the lists to class on the day you plan to conduct the activity.

Materials

- 9" x 12" white drawing paper
- pencils
- markers (fine-tipped)

Activity

1. Briefly discuss Universal Human Rights Month, and ask the children for some words that they feel describe this month. List these words on the chalkboard.

2. Explain that in this activity, we will be designing a large version of a selected word, composed of many small repeated copies of the same word. Demonstrate the process on the board, using a sample word, such as *care*.

3. Tell the children that they can think up their own words, use the words on the board, or choose from the list of words you provided. (distribute your word list at this point).

4. When they receive their drawing paper, ask the children to first lightly sketch the words they select in pencil. Remind them that the style can vary, and that the little words used to form the larger one can be written in script or printed. Encourage the kids to make their designs colorful.

5. Distribute the materials and let the fun begin.

6. When all the designs are complete, hold a discussion and exhibit.

Follow-Up

Invite the children to write short poems based on the words they selected. Display the poems with the word designs.

Helpful Books

- Greene, Laura. *Help: Getting to Know about Needing and Giving.* New York: Human Sciences Press, 1981.
- Hughes, Shirley. *Giving.* Cambridge, MA: Candlewick Press, 1993.

152

LOOKING AT SOME FREEDOMS

In America, we're very fortunate to have many freedoms that are not permitted in some other lands. Some of these include the freedom of speech, the freedom of the press, the freedom of religion, the freedom of expression, the freedom to receive an education, and the freedom to gather together. Although we often take such freedoms for granted, each one represents tremendous struggle and achievement in the cause of human rights.

This activity is devoted to examining some of the wonderful freedoms that we enjoy and to creating small sculptures to represent them. Before introducing the children to this topic, it's a good idea to sit back and think about a freedom that you cherish. Try to imagine what it would be like if that freedom were taken away, or were never available. After you have given this some thought, create a small plasticine sculpture that represents your idea of this freedom. When the sculpture is complete, bring it to school, and launch the topic with your students.

Materials

- 9" x 12" newsprint paper
- plasticine
- sticks
- plastic picnic utensils

Activity

1. Ask the children to name some of the freedoms that we enjoy in our country, and make a list of them on the chalkboard. They may need some help, so be ready to chime in if necessary.

2. Explain that in some places in the world, people are not allowed these freedoms. Ask the children if they have any stories to share about this issue.

153

3. Point out that in this activity, we will be choosing a freedom and making a small sculpture about it. Show the children your sculpture, and let them know that their creations can be formed in any style they wish: They can be realistic, abstract, expressionistic, symbolic, etc. They can also contain words inscribed into the plasticine.

4. Next, ask each child to carefully review the list of freedoms from the board and choose one that has meaning for him/her. Then, distribute the newsprint paper, plasticine, sticks, and plasticware, and let the children begin to work.

5. Be available to the children for discussion and consultation.

6. When all the sculptures are complete, hold a sharing session, and then exhibit the works in the school showcase.

Follow-Up

Ask the children to write an essay about the freedom they selected. You may wish to invite the parents to class for an essay reading and sculpture exhibit.

Helpful Books

• United Nations. *A Children's Chorus.* New York: Dutton, 1989.

154

BUILDING BRIDGES

Bridges are important because they bring two sides together. They unite two distinct places and make them one! In this activity, we will be creating simple, symbolic bridges that tie two countries together. The idea of building bridges to other places and between people is very important. With modern transportation and communications technology, our world is getting to be a smaller place. For this reason, it is vital that we cultivate better understanding between the different peoples of the Earth.

To complete this activity, we will be using a globe and an atlas. Just looking over these geographic materials should spark our curiosity about the amazing world we inhabit. Whether we choose a country where our ancestors lived or a place we know nothing at all about, building bridges builds excitement and interest.

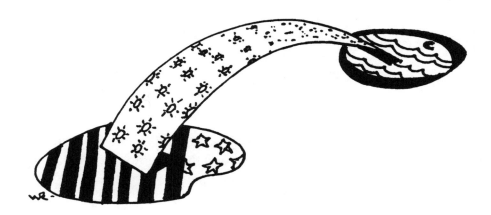

Materials

- 12" x 18" colored construction paper
- metallic paper
- wrapping paper scraps
- pencils
- crayons
- markers
- white glue
- scissors

Activity

1. Start this activity by asking the children some questions about bridges. What do bridges do? Why is it important to have bridges? Discuss these and related questions.

2. Explain that we will soon be creating symbolic bridges from our country to another country in the world. A globe or atlas can help us in this endeavor.

3. Briefly discuss the procedure for this activity by reviewing the following steps:

a. First, find a country on the globe or in the atlas, to which you would like to build a bridge. Remember that it could be a country where your relatives once lived, or where they still live.

b. Next, select several pieces of colored construction paper with which to work. Use one piece as a background and the others for cutting.

c. Draw and cutout two shapes in any design you wish. One of these shapes will represent our country: and the other, the country you selected. Decorate them, using the crayons and markers, and glue them into any position you wish on the 12" x 18" background sheet.

d. Next, cut a long strip of paper (length and width are up to each student), and gently bend it into position between the two shapes already glued in place. Make sure it creates a nice arch from one shape to the other. Unbend the arch, lay it flat on the tabletop, and decorate the strip with wrapping paper scraps, crayons, and markers.

e. Then, fold a 1" tab at each end of the strip, and glue one tab to our country, and the other to the country you selected. Your bridge is now complete.

4. Once the kids understand this process, dispense the materials, and let the construction begin.

5. When the colorful bridges are complete, hold a discussion and display.

Follow-Up

Invite the children to investigate the country they selected, and to give a brief report about it. Those children who selected the same place could do group reports.

Helpful Books

- Knowlton, Jack. *Maps & Globes.* New York: Thomas Y. Crowell, 1985.
- Rand McNally. *Children's World Atlas.* New York: Rand McNally, 1991.
- Tivers, Jacqueline, and Day, Michael. *The Viking Children's World Atlas: An Introductory Atlas for Young People.* New York: Viking Children's Books, 1994.

A BETTER WORLD

At one time or another, we've probably all thought about how our world could be a better place! Our newspapers, and television and radio broadcasts are too often filled with sad incidents that remind us of the many problems afflicting people around the world. Wars, famine, poverty, crime, and abuse pass before our eyes in a troubling procession. How can these horrible things be stopped? Why can't people live together more cooperatively and comfortably? These are but two questions that spring to mind.

In this activity, we are going to become sculptors of a sort, creating our vision of a better world. More specifically, we will be making mobiles that show some of the things that this "better world" might contain. If we envision a world filled with trees and flowers, for example, our mobile could be based on these natural images. Perhaps we will build a mobile composed of smiling faces from all over the globe, or one featuring pictures of good health care for all. The vision each of us has, and the theme selected, should be as individual as we are.

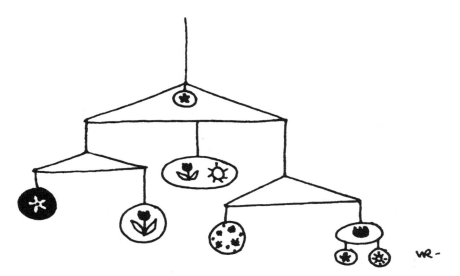

Materials

- composition paper
- pencils
- markers
- coat hangers
- string
- yarn
- colored posterboard
- colored construction paper and paper scraps
- scrap cardboard
- aluminum foil
- colored pipe cleaners
- found objects
- white glue
- scissors
- hole punches

Activity

1. Introduce the children to this activity by launching a discussion about our world and its many problems. Ask the children to imagine what their vision of a better world would be like.

2. Explain that each of us will be creating a mobile depicting our view of a better world. Remind students that a mobile is a moveable sculpture whose parts are usually set in motion by air currents.

3. Next, have the kids make a list on composition paper of some of the things a better world would contain.

4. Then, have them use the pencils to sketch their ideas on posterboard and cardboard, and the scissors to cut out the various shapes.

5. When all the shapes have been cut out, they can be decorated using construction paper, foil, markers, pipe cleaners, and found objects.

6. After the shapes are decorated, holes must be punched in each shape, so that string or yarn can be attached. The shapes can then be suspended and tied to the coat hangers. Remember to allow ample time for balancing the mobiles.

7. When all the mobiles are complete, hold a discussion and exhibit.

Follow-Up

Try to arrange to exhibit your class mobiles at the local public library. Ask the children to write poems or essays about their work, and display them alongside the mobiles.

Helpful Books

- Ryder, Willet. *The Art Experience.* Glenview, IL: GoodYearBooks, 1991.
- United Nations. *A Children's Chorus.* New York: Dutton, 1989.

LENDING A HELPING HAND

This activity involves putting words into action by actually lending a hand to a cause or organization concerned with human rights. The inspiration for this activity comes from two special grandmothers, Louise Ryder and Constance Siegel. By serving as fine examples in "lending a helping hand," they have influenced other family members to do likewise. I am also indebted to Eleanor Ryder and her fourth-grade students for providing a wonderful classroom model for this activity.

Class activities conducted by Mrs. Ryder and her students through the years have included raising money and creating puppets for a local orphanage, purchasing gift certificates at a local store for families in need, and writing letters to senior citizens who have no families of their own. The students have organized fairs, sung songs, held special sales, and donated their own money to make these things happen. As the year draws to a close, it is an appropriate time to take action in helping others.

Materials

- whatever it takes to put your plan into action!

Activity

1. To launch the activity, introduce the concept of "lending a helping hand" to your children. What does this idea mean? Can you give some examples?

2. List the examples which the children supply on the chalkboard. You might also wish to contribute some ideas of your own.

159

3. Explain to the children that we will be selecting one of the ideas listed and formulating a plan to help.

4. Next, hold a class vote to determine the most popular idea.

5. Once the idea has been chosen, you and your class can start to plan a strategy for lending a helping hand. If such a strategy involves fund-raising activities and/or agencies outside the school, be certain to consult with and obtain the permission of your school principal.

6. Conduct the activities you need to put your helping hands into action.

7. Take some photographs of your special project and send them to a local newspaper to inspire other classes to get involved.

Follow-Up

Invite the children to write a short story on "Lending a Helping Hand." Ask them to describe their feelings about helping other people.

Helpful Books

- Hughes, Shirley. *Alfie Gives a Hand.* New York: Lothrop, Lee & Shepard, 1983.
- Hughes, Shirley. *Giving.* Cambridge, MA: Candlewick Press, 1993.

From *Celebrating Diversity with Art: Thematic Projects for Every Month of the Year,* published by GoodYearBooks. Copyright © 1995 by Willet Ryder.